ECHOES OF
SILENCE

Spring Journal Books
Jungian Odyssey Series

Series Editors
Stacy Wirth
Isabelle Meier
John Hill

Other Titles in the Series

JUNGIAN ODYSSEY SERIES • VOLUME VI

ECHOES OF SILENCE

Listening to Soul, Self, Other

Series Editors
Ursula Wirtz
Stacy Wirth
Deborah Egger
Katy Remark

Consulting Editor
Nancy Cater

SPRING JOURNAL
BOOKS

PUBLICATIONS IN JUNGIAN PSYCHOLOGY
www.springjournalandbooks.com

Published by
Spring Journal, Inc.
New Orleans, Louisiana USA
www.springjournalandbooks.com

Spring Journal™, Spring: A Journal of Archetype and Culture™, Spring Books™, Spring Journal Books,™ Spring Journal and Books™, and Spring Journal Publications™ are all trademarks of Spring Journal Incorporated. All Rights Reserved.

Cover Photograph:
View of Kartause Ittingen from the East © Courtesy of Kartause Ittingen, Thurgau, Switzerland

Cover design and typography:
Northern Graphic Design and Publishing
info@ncarto.com

Text printed on acid-free paper

Library of Congress Cataloging-in-Publication Data Pending

Grateful acknowledgement is made to the respective publishers, institutions, and individuals for permission reprint as follows:

"Granum Sinapsis" by Anonymous, in *German Mystical Writings, Continuum*, © 2002 Karen J. Campbell, reprinted by permission of Bloomsbury Publishing Plc.

"Silence and Synchronicity in the Music of John Cage," by Craig E. Stephenson © 2013, printed by permission of the author.

Verdingkind [1], Kanton Bern 1940; Verdingkind [2], Kanton Bern 1940; Verdingkind with His Foster Father, Canton Bern 1946 (Verdingknabe mit seinem Pflegevater, Kanton Bern, 1946); and *Orphan Boy, Institutional Home Sonnenberg, Kriens 1944 (Heimknabe, Erziehungsanstalt Sonnenberg, Kriens, 1944),* all photographs by Paul Senn (1901-1953), reproduced by permission of Bernische Stiftung für Fotografie, Film und Video, Kunstmuseum Bern, Depositum Gottfried Keller-Stiftung, © Gottfried Keller-Stiftung, Bern.

Rowing and *Bodil Stefansson*, stills by Ingela Romare from her film *Rowing for Tranquility in Times of Burnout*, © 2010 Ingela Romare Myt & Bild, reproduced by permission of Ingela Romare.

Dr. Nokuzola Mndende at the IAAP Congress Cape Town 2007, still by Peter Ammann from his film *Healing in Two Worlds—Jungian Psychotherapists Encounter African Traditional Healers*, © 2008 Peter Ammann; *Bushpeople (San), A Healing Trance Dance*, still by Peter Ammann from his film *Spirits of the Rocks*, © 2002 Peter Ammann; and *Charmaine Joseph, In Durban, 2009*, photograph by Jane Bedford, © 2009 Jane Bedford; all images reproduced by permission of Peter Ammann.

Meditation

Jo Ann Hansen Rasch

My tongue is quiet
but chattering thoughts
challenge all serenity.

In the beginning was the word.
I seek what comes before this,
wait a lifetime for the answer.

Onto my path Soul throws out
a void of terrifying silence.
I become a pilgrim—step into emptiness

a poem greets me there.

(Inspired by the Jungian Odyssey
Kartause Ittingen, June 2013)

Contents

Acknowledgements

We are, as ever, indebted to Nancy Cater of Spring Journal Books, who has been quietly serving for many years as a member of the Jungian Odyssey Committee, standing steadily as an intimate consultant to our undertaking. Spring's endorsement of the Jungian Odyssey Series and the retreat itself has figured largely in making the Jungian Odyssey an event that welcomes participants from all around the world and from many different walks of life.

The Odyssey's rich program and smooth running relies always on the talents of many individuals. We wish to recognize our colleagues, too many to name here, who lead the morning meditations and the afternoon seminars and workshops. Unfortunately, limits of space prevent the inclusion of their contributions in the Jungian Odyssey Series. As ever, we are grateful to Helga Kopecky, ISAP's librarian, for keeping us well supplied with titles for our bookshop. Mary Tomlinson, a Canadian analyst and ISAP graduate (2011), continued, as she has done since 2006, to manage the individual course preferences. ISAP candidates, too, held forth with remarkable dedication: Susanne Bucher and Violetta Milutinovic kept apace with book sales; Ashish Pant, Natalia Lisenkova, and Naoko Nakamura provided technical support; Naoko served also as official photographer, capturing the week in vivid images that can be viewed by clicking "Photo Albums" at www.jungianodyssey.ch. Last, but certainly not least: our young friends and upcoming DJs Catherine Egger and Nadja Staub provided music for dancing at the closing gala dinner.

Ursula Wirtz, Deborah Egger,
Stacy Wirth, Katy Remark
Zürich April, 2014

Introduction

Echoes Of Silence
Listening To Soul, Self, Other

Ursula Wirtz and Stacy Wirth

> It is rewarding to watch patiently the silent happenings of the
> soul, and the most and best happens when it is not regulated
> from outside and above. . . . I readily admit that I have such
> great respect for what happens in the human soul that I would
> be afraid of disturbing and distorting the silent operation of
> nature by clumsy interference.
>
> —*C.G. Jung*[1]

By growing tradition, this volume collects the papers of scholars who lectured at ISAPZURICH'S annual Jungian Odyssey. It appeals to clinicians as well as to all others with interest in C.G. Jung's Analytical Psychology. Gathering in 2013 for our eighth event— now at Kartause Ittingen, now on the subject of silence—we were especially mindful of the inspiring *genius loci* and the particular paradox it posed. Our special guest speaker, the distinguished Jungian analyst Lionel Corbett, noted immediately the "irony of the situation," and quoted Lao Tzu, "Those who know, don't talk / those who talk, don't know."[2] To borrow from George Bernard Shaw, who expressed it with equal good humor, "I believe in the discipline of silence and could talk for hours about it."[3] More than hours, however, we devoted a whole week to talking about silence! While approaching the supreme mystery with words, music, film, and other images, we kept in mind Ludwig Wittgenstein's caution, "[w]hereof one cannot speak, thereof one must be silent."[4]

And so we immersed ourselves in this place of radical yet sublime simplicity and beauty, a former monastery founded in 1150. Lying in the rural lowlands of Canton Thurgau, it is some thirty miles (ca. fifty kilometers) from Jung's birthplace, Kesswil. Nestled amidst its own forests, farmlands, vineyards, and orchards, the monastery still distinctly echoes bygone centuries of existence as the tranquil refuge of a community of Carthusian monks. In 1524, at the hands of Protestant Reformists, the entire place was set in flames and silenced. Restoration was begun in 1531 when the Carthusian Order returned, to remain until 1868. As we learned,

> The monks took all meals except Sunday lunch alone in their cells, with each day divided into strict periods of work, rest and prayer (including a three-hour service every night from 11:30 pm, and never more than four-and-a-half hours' sleep at a stretch), and remaining committed by oath to silence at all times.[5]

We did not seek to emulate the monks' austerity—but we did hope to find the resonances at the core of our experience! Today Kartause Ittingen is run as a charitable foundation. Recently revived after a second major restoration, it is still rooted in the monastic tradition of quietude, self-sufficiency, and devotion to the nurture of mind, body, and soul. A home for the disabled provides training programs and work at Ittingen's own farm, vineyard, dairy, brewery, distillery, charcoal kiln, pottery shop, hotel, and restaurant. The fruits of their endeavors graced our tables each day: fresh-baked bread, homemade cheese and yogurt, fragrant *eaux-de-vie* and cider distilled onsite, homegrown vegetables, home-brewed Klosterbräu beer made from handpicked hops.

Among this Odyssey's special events was a trip to the historic old town of St. Gallen, which evolved from a hermitage founded in the seventh century. In 1983, swaths of it were designated a UNESCO

World Heritage Site. Strolling along the narrow cobblestone streets, and admiring the often whimsically decorated timber-beamed homes, we stopped to visit the Cathedral, the Abbey, and the Abbey Library. Dating to 820 AD, the library itself is Switzerland's oldest. We were privileged to linger in the Baroque hall that makes this also one of the most beautiful libraries in the world. Close-up views of medieval illuminated manuscripts took our breath away. At St. Lawrence Church, a basilica in neo-Gothic style, a number of stout souls mounted many stone steps to arrive at the top of the tower, obtaining a panoramic view of old St. Gallen's rooftops.

During the Odyssey lectures, seminars, and workshops that took place within Ittigen's cloister walls (sheep bleating outside our windows), we each replaced for awhile the noise of civilization (and the noise of our otherwise rather buoyant conference!). Now and then we tarried, finding solitude in the lush gardens of roses, hops, and herbs. Some wandered into the old monks' cells, or the fine arts museum, or even beyond, into the forest. In the stunning Baroque cloister church, we listened to a solo concert by the Swiss flutist Heironymus Schädler.[6] ISAP analyst Verena Bollag treated us to intermittent piano solos. Midway through the week, a sudden and wild thunderstorm swept through our fondue night at the forest's edge—rewarding those who braved it out with a full rainbow shimmering against a quiet, eerily lit evening sky. Might this have been an intuited sacred wind, arriving to inspirit our sailing through unknown waters to the yet unknown shores of the great silence?

The authors in this volume follow the Odyssey itself, as if bearing in mind the familiar proverb, "speech is silver; silence is golden." They point to an alchemical *coniunctio* of silver and gold, a joining of opposites that can give us the wisdom to know when to speak and when to listen deeply—when to observe the season for speech, when to abide by the season for silence. Their essays bid us to explore the silence that underlies the chattering mind, often revealing itself as the great teacher and guide to one's innermost core and truth. We discover bodily journeys that lead us on the way, and music that resounds with no sound. But we are asked to listen to the textures—what is the meaning of silence in psychotherapy and analysis? Can we echo in our hearts the silence that traps the oppressed and exploited? When is silence healing, and when does it crush us? Can we speak out about what truly matters? Indeed one author begs, "make more noise!" Thus readers of this volume are invited to re-imagine and re-create themselves, to respond to the challenges of the soul's beckoning, to try to attune to the echoes of the Self.

As we enter the chapters to come, so do we also enter into the spirit of the place, the chambers of the heart, and Jung's reflection, "It is rewarding to watch patiently the silent happenings of the soul . . . ." Following Ralph Waldo Emerson, let us take the time—even while reading so many words—to "wait,"

> —to hear the whisper of the gods. Let us not interfere. . . . Wait, and thy heart shall speak. Wait, until the necessary and everlasting overpowers you, until day and night avail themselves of your lips.[7]

—on behalf of the Jungian Odyssey Committee
Ursula Wirtz, Academic Chair
Deborah Egger, Co-Chair
Stacy Wirth, Co-Chair
Katy Remark, Internuncio
Nancy Cater, Honorary Advisor

NOTES

[1] C.G. Jung, "Individual Dream Symbolism in Relation to Alchemy"[1944], in *Psychology and Alchemy, The Collected Works of C.G Jung*, 2nd Ed., Bollingen Series XX, trans. R.F.C Hull (Princeton, NJ: University of Princeton Press, 1968), Vol. 12, § 126.

[2] Lionel Corbett, "Silence, Presence, and Witness in Psychotherapy," in this volume.

[3] George Bernard Shaw, No. 10578, in *Dictionary of Quotations*, ed. Connie Robertson (Hertfordshire: Wordsworth Editions, Ltd., 1998), p. 391.

[4] Ludwig Wittgenstein, *Tractatus Logico-Philosophicus*, International Library of Psychology, Philosophy, and Scientific Method, general ed. C.K. Odgen (London: Kegan Paul, Trench, Truber & Co. Ltd., 1922), p. 23.

[5] *Switzerland is Yours*, Micheloud & Cie, 2103, at http://areyours.com/e/guide/northeast/kartause.html (accessed 14 April, 2014).

[6] Heironymus Schädler, an awarded musician and composer, is known for unusual programs built on his commitment to bridge with other arts forms, including literature, dance, painting, and nature as well. He has performed in Europe, the US, and elsewhere around the world. For further information see, http://www.hieronymusik.li (in German only; accessed 14 April, 2014).

[7] Ralph Waldo Emerson, "Friendship" [1841], *The Essays of Ralph Waldo Emerson* (Harvard University Press, 1987), p. 124.

1

Silence, Presence, and Witness in Psychotherapy

Lionel Corbett

INTRODUCTION

As I begin to reflect on silence, I cannot help remembering Lao Tzu's words, "Those who know, don't talk / Those who talk, don't know."[1] I can therefore only appeal to the irony of the situation in which I find myself. To further illustrate the paradox that silence presents when we try to talk about it, I can do no better than to quote the Persian poet and Sufi mystic Rumi, who wrote a great deal about silence. He says, "A great silence overcomes me, and I wonder why I ever thought to use language."[2] He asks,

> Why are you so afraid of silence,
> silence is the root of everything.
> If you spiral into its void,
> a hundred voices will thunder messages you long to hear.[3]

When Rumi was asked why he wrote so much about silence, he replied, "The radiant one inside me has never said a word."[4] However, he also said of a poem, "This song came out of silence and is being authored by silence." So here is the paradox he articulates: the Self is silent, but everything emerges from that silence.

Silence is therefore not something negative; it is not just an absence of sound or a pause between words. Silence is a non-conceptual mode of knowing.[5] There is a nonverbal stream of experience that cannot be spoken, a stream which is going on alongside the kind of experience that can be spoken of. To attain inward silence is to listen to the voice within, which is the voice of the Self. Perhaps this is why, in a letter dated May 30, 1957, Jung writes, "Solitude is a fount of healing which makes my life worth living. Talking is often a torment for me, and I need many days of silence to recover from the futility of words."[6] Hence the importance to Jung of his Bollingen tower.

Silence has an amazing number of qualities and textures; it can be eloquent and full of emotion; it can be pregnant, indifferent, awkward, threatening, cold, angry, ecstatic, or empty; it can be used as a form of power, a way to ostracize and control, or a way to honor and remember. Silence can be used to heal when we are totally receptive to the other, or it can be used as a weapon, to be arrogant or demeaning or to ostracize. Silence can produce fear, because words are a form of control of oneself and others. We use words to justify ourselves.

Perhaps the Self can best be experienced in silence, which is why all the contemplative spiritual traditions practice silence and solitude. These traditions all seek the non-conceptual Awareness that is the Ground of being, and the heightened sense of interiority that silence allows. In eastern traditions, meditative practices are often called the paths of silence; the Sufi guide is often referred to as a "silent physician." Since meditative silence points to the Self, silence is itself a true symbol. As we practice silence and solitude, we discover an internal awareness that is usually obscured by the noise of the outer world. This awareness is not discursive but it is intensely meaningful.

Because we may experience the Self intensely in solitude and silence, many spiritual traditions speak of the need for silence for spiritual development or to allow the divine to enter the heart. Some traditions think of revelation by means of the Word, but sometimes the Self speaks in a silence more profound than words. In the Bible, after Elijah has been victorious in his contest with the prophets of Baal, he is forced to escape the wrath of Jezebel by hiding in the desert. He experiences a wind that broke rocks in pieces, an earthquake, and a fire, but the Lord was not in any of these; Elijah then hears what is traditionally translated as a "still small voice,"[7] but which is translated in the New Revised Standard Version as "a sound of sheer silence." I am reminded here of the words of St. Paul, who says that the Spirit intercedes with "sighs too deep for words."[8] That is, there is a level of emotion during which the Self is present but its response is too deep for words. Perhaps this "too deep for words" feeling compelled Rilke to write, "Things aren't so tangible and sayable as people would usually have us believe; most experiences are unsayable, they happen in a space that no word has ever entered."[9] The poets of course know what it is like when words fail us; as T.S. Eliot confessed, ". . . Words strain / Crack and sometimes break, under the burden, / . . . / Decay with imprecision, will not stay in place."[10] It is easier to be silent if we trust that an underlying transcendent reality is ordering the situation; silence is then an affirmation of faith. That is why Krishnamurti observes,

> And it is only where there is space and silence that something new can be that is untouched by time/thought. That may be the most holy, the most sacred—*may* be. You cannot give it a name. It is perhaps the unnamable.[11]

We call this the Self. Similarly, perhaps, Meister Eckhart emphasizes, "Silence is a privileged entry into the realm of God . . . there is a huge silence inside each of us that beckons us to itself. . . . there is nothing in the world that resembles God as much as silence."[12] It is not surprising that the mystics of all traditions believe that Silence is the ground of Reality. Lao Tzu, for instance, says,

> The myriad things flourish
> And each one returns to its root.
> Returning to the root is silence.
> Silence is returning to being.[13]

This is the silence from which being emerges; it is the source, the silence at the root of existence.

There is an important connection between silence and religious faith. For Kierkegaard, the silence of Abraham when he is commanded to sacrifice his son Isaac is the beginning of the fear of God—fear and trembling condemn Abraham to faithful silence.[14] Something similar happens in the biblical story of Aaron's two sons who are killed because they come too close to the Holy of Holies, "And Aaron was silent."[15] The Talmud tells a story in which Moses was told by God to be silent. In a vision, God showed him the future generations of the Jewish people, and the leaders of each generation. Moses was greatly impressed by the wisdom of Rabbi Akiva, but he also saw the way the Romans tortured Akiva to death. Moses therefore asked God, "Is this the reward of his Torah knowledge?" God answered, "Be silent; thus it arose in My thought."[16] Silence is always present as a background to our activity—we are surrounded by silence. In meditation, silence becomes a palpable presence, and everything emanates from silence. Unfortunately we are habituated to noise, which deafens us to this underlying silence. Perhaps this is not surprising; as the seventeenth-century philosopher and mathematician Blaise Pascal disclosed, "the eternal silence of these infinite spaces fills me with dread."[17] (He was referring to the feeling of smallness in the face of infinity.) Pascal also suggested that the cause of our unhappiness is our inability to stay quietly in a room.

Silence can act as a kind of barrier that prevents intrusion into one's privacy. But silence can be very uncomfortable just because it prevents the defensive use of words. The ability to share silence is a form of intimacy and self-revelation; silence is then a form of communication. When a person is most deeply moved, he or she is often silent. Silence can be very frightening, partly because it is an intimation of eternity and partly because we associate it with absence; perhaps silence echoes our fearful childhood experience of being left alone at bedtime, separated from mother and the rest of the family.

Some experiences cannot be spoken of, or we alter them when we try to speak of them; language belongs to the realm of ego, to dualisms such as subject-object dichotomies. Language is not good at communicating the more subtle realms of subjectivity that we call soul. Or, simply put, silence facilitates contact with the unconscious. The ego is a conditioned mind, but silence allows an experience of the unconditioned mind, of the pure awareness which is the Self. The important thing about the silence of pure awareness is that there is nothing that needs to be done to get it; it just is, always infinitely present. We have been conditioned to think we need religious systems and belief systems in order to be in touch with transpersonal awareness, but this is not so; the silence of the Self is immediately available as a felt sense in the body. This silence is nothing-ness—it is not an entity. Thoughts and feelings or the everyday mind emerge spontaneously out of this silence, which is the Self as the fabric of the universe. Silence is like light that reveals what is inside us, so that by being silent, we see the ego working, wanting, complaining, searching for some holy grail that we think will make us happy, but if we wait in silence the ego falls away. The resulting silence allows us to pay attention to the sensation of being, which is at a different level than the level of activity. Silence opens us to the Self, and with practice, one begins to realize that the silence of the Self is behind all the words and activity, which is why Rumi is reported to have said, "Silence is the language that God speaks and everything else is a bad translation."

In art, silence is the negative space; in music, the pause between notes; in poetry, what is left to the imagination. Without the silence between notes, there would be no music, just a constant hum or total chaos; we need alternating periods of silence and sound to produce meaningful patterns and rhythms. Without the silence between words, there would be just confused babbling. Without empty space in art we would not see shape. Both music and art convey a silent message to the observer, or sometimes an emotion that cannot be put into words. In one of his last letters to Freud, Jung ends by saying, "The rest is silence," which are also the final words of Hamlet as he dies. Hamlet had been visited by his father's ghost, who wants Hamlet to avenge his father's killer.[18] Given the father-son aspects of the Freud-Jung relationship, perhaps Jung's allusion to silence here tells us something of what was in his mind without his having to articulate it.

Silence in Psychotherapy

Silence is not just an absence of sound; it is a presence and a quality of mind and heart that allows deep listening, so that silence is important for psychotherapy. Psychotherapy is supposed to be the talking cure, but silence is an important aspect of the process of psychotherapy. Silence and deep listening without comment or judgment foster compassion and understanding; the patient knows when this has happened. Silence has texture; during periods of silence in therapy we empathically feel the other person's emotional life. We tend to listen to the words, but the silences are sometimes more evocative. Silence has many flavors; it can indicate confusion when the patient or therapist does not know what to say, or silence can be withholding because of shame or anger. At moments, silence is a gift that means nothing needs to be said.

Silence in psychotherapy has its own relational qualities and can have many meanings. Much of the psychoanalytic literature ignores the creative and integrative function of silence. Only a few authors talk about silence as a form of deepening of the therapeutic bond, or as an expression of an intrapsychic *coniunctio*. Sacha Emanuel Nacht points out that there are some exchanges between analyst and patient that only occur in silence; there is a deep inner attitude of the therapist that is more important than words—what Jung described as unconscious to unconscious communication.[19] However, the patient's silence is often understood as a resistance, which was Freud's opinion, as a destructive attack on the therapy or as the result of shame, fear, spite,[20] or anger (according to Arlow[21]). Silence may also be a meaningful communication, a way of relating, a regressive fusion with the therapist, or a power play. Silence may mean that the patient is possessed by a powerful complex that renders him speechless. In 1926, in a lecture to the Vienna Psychoanalytic Society (which took 42 years to be published), Theodor Reik suggested that behind a fear of silence lies the unconscious fear of a loss of love, and so people speak because they cannot bear silence.[22] Ralph Greenson proposed that silence with open eyes is more likely to be the result of hatred and rejection, while silence with closed eyes derives from love and acceptance.[23] Sometimes only the therapist's countertransference helps us decide among such a variety of possibilities.

In fact the patient's silence *stimulates* the therapist's countertransference. During silences the therapist may feel helpless or shut out, angry or frustrated or bored, all of which give us a clue as to the patient's inner life. A concordant countertransference may tell us how the patient was made to feel in childhood, perhaps afraid to speak in the presence of a hostile parent. In turn, within the transference the patient may experience the therapist's silence as either warm and supportive or as cold and hostile. The patient may need the therapist to be silent so he can gather his thoughts and feelings and find a way to talk about them. There is a felt difference between sitting with someone who is silently collecting his thoughts and a silence that is defensive and anxious. The patient may be silent because he is afraid the therapist will not understand how he feels. Silence can be used to preserve self-esteem, or as a way of controlling one's feelings, or to maintain a feeling of self-sufficiency. Shame produces silence, or silence hides shame. In these situations, the therapist has to wonder what the person cannot say; the therapist has to grasp intuitively what is communicated non-verbally or what can only be grasped through feeling or empathy. The patient's silence can show us what it was like to be with a depressed mother who would not speak; sometimes when this is repeated in the therapy we find ourselves drifting off into our own concerns. Or silence can simply be a form of respite. The patient may need isolation to preserve a part of her sense of self, and may therefore dislike the therapist's intrusion. In patients who have been massively traumatized or who have insecure attachment, silence may protect a vital core of the self. Of course, the therapist's silence can be a form of countertransference based on her own material, or a form of counter-resistance.

Because silence forces the therapist to *feel* or intuit what is not expressed, the therapeutic problem is one of discernment, because often we do not know the meaning of a particular period of silence. We know there are wordless overtones going on between patient and therapist, but we do not know how to read meaning from what is not said. We don't know whether to allow the silence because the patient needs space and time, or whether we should try to help the person say something it is hard to say. If the analyst speaks, will it feel intrusive and controlling? If we are silent, will this feel like an abandonment? Is it OK to say something about the patient's body language? This discernment can be difficult, and if we make some kind of interpretation because we think the silence is controlling or hostile, the interpretation may sound accusatory or shaming and so make things worse. When dreams occur, they may be helpful; a dream in which a woman is swimming under a frozen ocean and could not find a spot to surface told me about her subjective experience. Sometimes the therapist counters the patient's silence with his own silence as a way of forcing the patient to speak—but the therapist's silence can feel like abandonment if the patient has separation anxiety. In childhood, bedtime often means separation from mother, so silence is often unconsciously associated with separation anxiety, for both participants. Sometimes silence is such a strain on the therapist that the therapist tries to nag a silent patient into speaking. The therapist's silence at the wrong time can be devastating for the patient—it may feel persecutory—while to be silent at the right time can be very helpful.

The problem with silence in psychotherapy is therefore twofold; one is the need for patient waiting on the part of the therapist, the other is how to judge the quality of a silent period, since we know that there are times when we must not speak. However, it is important that silence not be used as a deliberate tool or technique; to be authentic, silence must arise spontaneously in the therapeutic field. Nina Coltart points out that the observation of silence in therapy is a two-way process: the patient studies the analyst's silence as much as the analyst studies the patient's silence, and if the analyst is irritated or angry, the patient will detect these feelings, so one has to practice benevolent patience and observe peacefully.[24]

BEARING WITNESS

There are occasions in psychotherapy when one can only silently and helplessly witness the suffering of another person, when there is nothing in the books or in our imagination that helps us with the situation we are facing. Witnessing is an archetypal human process. People need to give testimony to their experience, and one of the important functions of the psychotherapist is to act as a witness to what has happened. Witnessing is not a passive process; it means that we empathically grasp the emotional significance of what is being said, and we are much affected by it, but we do not interfere. This silence is quite different than withdrawal; it is active presence, allowing the soul to speak. I believe that if we are truly silent and fully present at these times, we can feel the presence of the Self in the room.

We cannot witness without at the same time participating. The act of witnessing seems to catalyze the patient's experience, or sometimes allows something to be experienced that otherwise would remain inchoate. Sometimes traumatized people suffer in isolation because they have been unable to speak about their experience, and their soul longs for a healing witness. Psychotherapeutic witnessing adds meaning to the patient's experience. Sometimes a person does not know what he or she feels, or cannot make sense of something about themselves, until what they feel is said in the presence of another; witnessing then allows the patient to really believe that what he or she says is valid. This is not simply about offering comfort. It *matters* to people that someone else recognizes and deeply understands how they feel and what has happened to them, even if nothing can be done about it. Nor is this merely a (mirror) transference phenomenon. As important as the transference is, when the therapist is silently witnessing a patient's anguish the therapist is a real person, not only a transference figure. Being seen in a meaningful way helps the process of self-development and individuation—and I believe that silent witnessing of the suffering of another person benefits the therapist as much as the patient. In a way, silent presence is the opposite pole to interpretation or actively working on a dream. But at the same time, working on a dream is an act of witness to the unconscious, which may also wish to be seen, which may be one reason it produces dreams. Perhaps the unconscious needs a witness, or as Jung says, a reflecting consciousness in the human ego.

Witnessing might be particularly important if the psychotherapist is working with someone who has been the victim of evil. In a way the psychotherapist then stands in for society as a whole, acknowledging that this should not have happened. If the witness-therapist can help to contain the pain of these memories, related memories emerge and they become better able to be integrated in the presence of a therapist. Sometimes we are privileged to witness the emergence of an aspect of the person's soul that has long been unavailable; sometimes we can witness a truth about the person that he or she cannot see him or herself. This often requires silence on the part of the therapist, which may require a sacrifice on the part of the therapist on behalf of the patient—the sacrifice of an interpretation or the sacrifice of a demonstration of the therapist's knowledge. An unobtrusive, holding silence, combined with the therapist's emotional investment, are required for witnessing what the soul wishes to say. "Holding" here means allowing space for feelings to emerge in a way that feels contained and safe. The *temenos* of the therapy room is one of the few places in our culture where this may happen.

Witnessing may be an important part of the healing effects of therapy. The act of witness is an act of caring that makes us feel vulnerable and opens the psychotherapist to the unknown; it requires

courage, because we have no idea what may emerge. We empathically
sense terror, rage, and helplessness, and we must respond in a way that
signifies we are affected but not overwhelmed. It is painful to see a
person's extreme vulnerability, but this must not be avoided, although
it sometimes leads to detachment in therapists who cannot tolerate it
because it stirs up too much of the therapist's vulnerability. To stay
with the suffering of the other person is to suffer oneself; suffering
invariably stimulates our own vulnerability and our own difficulties.
At the same time, we have to be careful to manage our own feelings
and not burden the patient with them by inducing in the patient an
obligation to look after the witness. Nevertheless, one cannot help but
imagine oneself in a similar situation. Sometimes the best we can do
is to be a companion in the person's suffering, without the sense that
we are trying to take away his or her pain, rather than think we are
trying to "treat" the person in the usual sense.

True witnessing is not detached; to witness is to take in as fully as
possible what is going on with the other and to be a part of what is
going on, which is an act of mercy and love. The therapist's silent
caring is an act of love, which may be all we can do to alleviate
suffering. This love is transmitted silently by means of one's
presence, one's facial expression, and one's eyes. The face is very
important (an argument not to use a couch) because even if the
therapist is silent, the patient perceives subtle changes in the
therapist's face, which tell the patient that he is affecting the
therapist, and we need to feel that we can affect others. We take a
risk when we witness silently; we face great uncertainty, but we may
discover something very important; a new understanding and new
values may emerge. Somehow, the act of witnessing itself expresses an
important human value. I hope the philosopher Emmanuel Levinas
is correct when he says that to stand before another person and say
"here I am" is to act as a witness of the good, the Infinite, or God.[25]
According to Levinas, the face of the other awakens an ethical
responsibility in us and a wish to care for the other. To be a witness is
to truly see the other in all his vulnerability, a vulnerability which itself
evokes our own sense of responsibility and personal vulnerability
toward the other. Levinas believes that when a person is at the disposal
of another, he witnesses that there is "something beyond," a witness
to the eternal. One is then a witness to goodness. He believes as well

that such witnessing has a spiritual character, provided that the witness is in contact with his or her own connection to the spirit. Then, witnessing is the witnessing of goodness, eternity, and the Infinite. For Levinas, to care for the other's suffering before one's own is the height of a person's humanity, the highest form of human selfhood, and an ethical imperative. For him, it is incumbent on me to respond properly to the suffering of another person. Levinas therefore describes a form of spirituality in which one might be able to see infinity in the face of the other; this face points to the beyond. The absolute otherness of the other person cannot be grasped or understood, and so opens the door to infinity. The face of the other makes the otherness of the other concrete; this otherness is essential to witnessing. Looking at the face of the other, being separate and caring, and understanding the meaning of the other's suffering, are all one.

An interesting paradox about the process of silent witnessing in psychotherapy is that it reflects the patient's ability to differentiate himself from the therapist, to individuate, but at the same time to experience a deep level of connection. These should not be thought of as opposites; they are part of a unitary process of development. We are alone with our difficulties but present with the other at the same time.

There is of course a dark side to the process of witnessing; not everyone is able to listen to serious emotional pain or trauma, and sometimes the witness feels he must say something because he cannot keep silent and has to offer advice. Or the unhelpful witness wants to minimize or deflect the severity of the sufferer's pain, which makes the sufferer feel even more isolated and hopeless. In other words, talking about trauma without being properly received and witnessed is itself traumatic.

PRESENCE IN PSYCHOTHERAPY: PRESENCE AS SPIRITUAL ATTENTION

A little more Rumi:

> There is a way between voice and presence where information flows.
> In disciplined silence it opens.
> With wandering talk it closes.[26]

People get something important from psychotherapy, but not necessarily anything verbal; silent presence is a powerful medicine. Presence is essential for meaningful psychotherapy to occur, and presence may be present even if we are silent. However, therapeutic presence is elusive and hard to describe. It is possible to be physically present but not psychologically or spiritually present. There seems to be something more about presence than the presence of the body; presence seems to extend beyond the body, like a spiritual extension of the body. Presence is something that comes and goes, and we can be aware if it is present or not—we can detect it in people who are available and open. Presence is conveyed by tone of voice, facial expression, body language, and gesture; it is an offering of oneself. Presence is not the same as charisma; charismatic people do have presence, but one can be present without charisma, and charisma can feel like a narcissistic form of presence. Presence is not passive; it requires strength to be present to suffering. The therapist can enhance his or her presence by focusing on the breath, on one's state of muscle tension, and on a sense of internal stillness and awareness. I believe one then is in touch with the Self in the body, and this has an effect on the other person who is moved towards his own sense of this presence. We then sense the presence of the Self in each other.

Some people seem to have a healing presence, something that induces an experience of peace, comfort, or well-being in suffering people. Some of this is about the capacity for empathy, compassion, and the spirituality of the healer. However, healing presence has not been well studied, or it has been dismissed as part of the placebo effect— what we might call the constellation of the inner healer. Most healing traditions assume the effect of a transpersonal or spiritual component that is independent of the subject's cognitive processes. When healers are asked for the components of healing, they list: love, spiritual grace, focused awareness, openness to healing, creativity, imagination, relatedness, intention, belief, direction of energy, listening, and reconciliation.[27] Love provides the force; intention provides the direction of the force. True healing presence may require that we are aware of the spiritual level of the therapeutic relationship—the presence of the Self.

There are various aspects of presence in psychotherapy; the presence of the therapist and the presence of the Self. For me, the presence of intense emotion indicates the presence of the Self in the therapy room, because the Self incarnates itself by means of the emotion of the complex, so that emotion is the Self felt in the body.

By tracking the person's emotion, we follow the archetype at the center of the complex into the body. Allowing a somatic resonance in the therapist's body, the therapist becomes an additional container for the patient's intensely powerful affects, which inevitably resonate with our own material. The capacity to contain the patient's painful affects is helped if the therapist has been able to contain similar affective states. If one has been through one's own terror or despair, one can non-verbally communicate this to the patient, and this contact allows one to meet the other in the deepest core of the soul. This ability to be with the other, to contain without repression, acting out, or retaliation, has a deep impact. Very often, the only meaningful response to the analysand's intense emotion is silence. Words would not do justice to the pain that is going on, and we realize we are part of a much larger process that we cannot fully understand. Silence emerges because we know that there is nothing the ego can say or do; one can only be a witness to the moment.

The presence of the therapist has been regarded as one of the most important aspects of psychotherapy—even healing in its own right, even essential to the therapeutic relationship (see for example Shari Geller and Leslie Greenberg,[28] and Orah Krug[29]). Presence is important to all schools of psychotherapy, but the exact nature of presence is not clear. One definition is that therapeutic presence is the state of having one's whole self in the encounter on many levels—physical, cognitive, emotional, and spiritual all at the same time, so that one is attuned and responsive, with a "kinesthetic and emotional sensing of the other's affect and experience as well as one's own intuition and skill and the relationship between them."[30] One has to empty oneself to be fully present: by emptying oneself, one allows an internal space inside oneself that allows one to be filled with the presence of the other. Presence is not about what we do or say in psychotherapy; it is about how we are with the other person. Many writers believe that the way the therapist is present in the therapy room reflects the way that person is in his or her life. Presence means being available and open to all aspects of experience, one's own and that of the other, and the capacity to respond from this experience. Presence is clearly more important than the therapist's theoretical orientation. To be present one has to let go of one's knowledge and experience, one's presuppositions, diagnoses, and so on. One has to be absorbed, fully in the moment with no goal in mind, only interest and attention. This diminution of the hegemony of the ego allows the Self to be felt in the room.

Non-dual presence means the realization that it is the same Self in both of us, and that at the deepest level we are not separate. For this, we must allow ourselves to be totally affected by what is happening. We listen with close attention, without judgment, not trying to make something happen. Non-dual presence produces a sense of timelessness and lack of spatial boundaries. When one is truly present, one feels psychologically as if one is physically very close to the other person, even though there is the usual physical space between us. The moment is timeless; the whole of one's past is here and now, in the moment. This kind of deep listening means that we are fully present, but not listening for anything in particular, and we are not interpreting or needing something to happen. This is a kind of unconditioned listening, without a theoretical listening "perspective." It makes one realize how attached we are to talking.

Some contemporary psychoanalysts are developing the idea that there are other transformative experiences in therapy beside verbal interpretation and a focus on the past. Daniel Stern writes about special moments of meeting or "now" moments in psychotherapy, when something special happens that has a big impact on the treatment or which transforms the way the therapist and patient are with each other.[31] These moments offer the greatest potential for authenticity and change; this is where the "magic in a therapy session or in intimate relationships" resides.[32] From a Jungian viewpoint, this happens when we sense the presence of the numinosum in the therapy room; these "moments of meeting" are actually moments of sacred presence. Sometimes these moments are almost imperceptible, when we suddenly and unexpectedly grasp something that is said, something of special importance. These are moments with a core of feeling that cannot always be put into words; often they are *silent* moments in which we feel direct access to the quality of the other soul. The relational field suddenly changes. During these moments we are both equally vulnerable. Sometimes an important dream may follow such a moment. During these moments, theory is at a distance; only the immediate connection is important, not cognitive meaning. A present moment is very brief, requiring narrow but intense focus. Attention to these micro-moments is a radical change from the broader focus of classical psychoanalysis with its emphasis on the past and on making the unconscious conscious.

SILENT MENTAL PAIN

There are types of mental pain that simply cannot be put into words. Mental pain of this kind can be distinguished from psychological suffering.[33] Mental pain means a diffuse, unpleasant emotional state, sometimes felt as bodily sensations that seem to make no sense, that cannot be put into words or symbolized, and so cannot be communicated to another person. This pain cannot be "mentalized," so that we cannot name it, we cannot give it an image or find a metaphor to express it. We may feel mental pain as vague sensations in the chest or abdomen, yet we know it does not result from a bodily problem—we know it is something psychological, or something on the border of the mental and physical. Mental pain may be an inchoate form of longing, helplessness, or despair that cannot be elaborated; it is different than suffering which can be named, described, talked about, and elaborated, for instance by the work of mourning. As we elaborate suffering in these ways we become better able to tolerate and contain it. Suffering, such as that due to the loss of a vital selfobject, is somewhat relieved when it is talked about and grieved normally. However, mental pain occurs because the person cannot put into words how she feels, and can only talk about distress that has no name—it is not a clearly defined emotion. The therapist feels this in the countertransference as intense but inchoate distress, sometimes somatic. Mental pain occurs when a person lacks the capacity to suffer consciously—there are forms of mental pain that have no name. In Bion's language, mental pain is the result of toxic beta elements derived from traumatic experiences that cannot be symbolized or given meaning.[34] In contrast, true psychic suffering is the result of a negative experience that can be tolerated and symbolized by the "alpha function" of the mental apparatus.

Mental pain is so unbearable it often leads to a variety of defensive maneuvers. Psychic retreat or withdrawal may occur, either leading to an attempt to discover what is going on and mourn as necessary, or to a hopeless giving up on relationships in general. Denial is a form of psychic numbing, or manic defense may occur with feverish over-activity such as overwork or multiple sexual encounters used to avoid feeling the pain of loss. Alternatively, mental pain can be induced in others, sometimes by projective identification, or it can be acted out physically by self-mutilation. The use of a creative outlet is an important way of managing mental pain; there is a well-known relationship between loss and creativity. The psychoanalyst Salman Ahktar believes that poetry is a particularly effective way of processing emotional pain because it allows all the defenses mentioned above.[35] Reading or writing allows withdrawal of attention from one's surroundings, or a psychic retreat; it allows mental work as a form of manic defense. The traumatic event is changed into a creative product, and the writer's pain is shared with an imaginary audience with whom the poet is in dialog. For Ahktar, poetry has direct access to the deepest levels of the psyche, which is where mental pain resides; poetry speaks to the unconscious directly, informs the person of the internal state of affairs, and facilitates both mourning and mentalization of non-verbal levels of the psyche.

SILENCE AND NONDUALITY

Nonduality is a spiritual philosophy found in many traditions that teach that reality is an undivided unity; there is no separation between people or between people and the world. Jung's idea that the Self is a totality and is the same in all of us, is a psychological statement of this idea.

Receptive silence in psychotherapy invokes a special quality of experience in which there is no you and me, no division between us. In that space the Self is present as pure awareness, beyond thought. If we are truly silent and open, a process may happen which Krishnamurti calls "insight into what-is."[36] Here the word "insight" is not used in the traditional psychoanalytic sense, where it refers to understanding the dynamics of one's conflicts; i.e., where insight is considered to be a function of the synthesizing and integrating capacity of the ego which occurs as a result of the return of repressed material that is now accepted by the ego, leading to a psychic reorganization. All this sounds mechanical. Rather, insight in Krishnamurti's sense is a totally new and fresh perception of the way things actually are, not based on previous knowledge, but an instantaneous grasp and inward awareness that involves the whole body and mind. Therefore, the presence of theory in the therapist's mind actually prevents the arising of real insight because the mind would then only see what it already knows is there.

Periods of silence in psychotherapy are a potential entrance into non-dual awareness; we are both complete in some deep way, and our ego stories fade into the background. Staying silent but connected in this way can be a healing experience. It is important to have no preferences at these moments; we may hope that the silence ends or that it continues, but either way it is an ego intrusion, the kind of preference that will affect what happens. Non-dual silence is something that happens, not something that we do.

When I do see the other clearly, the space between us disappears, or at least I am not conscious of it. There is just the field; no observer and observed, just hopes and fears, rage, pain, ambition, envy, deadness, and so on that we are both experiencing. I may experience the quality of this field either imaginally, somatically, or as a certain energetic quality in the room. I do not need to call "my" experience a projective identification, since there is no real boundary across which projection has occurred. If we think in theoretical terms, a subjective space has arisen between us, producing an observer and an observed. I am then not totally involved, and concepts occupy that space. Words and concepts, my likes and dislikes, prevent real perception of the other. Only total attention within the field allows clear seeing, and then love can be present.

Clear perception removes the wall of separation between us and allows real understanding. When I understand, I can see something about the "other" that cannot be put into words, but is so vital, so true about the other that I feel it totally. This does not happen if I am trying to apply a theory. If I have a theory I know what *should be* rather than what actually *is*, and I see the other ideologically. A real danger of analysis is that to analyze another person implies that we are separate, meaning there is no actual contact, and consequently neither real relationship nor union. Analysis is the response of my knowledge and technique, my accumulated learning and experience rather than a response to what is in front of me. The notion of "listening perspectives" in psychotherapy is therefore pernicious; a theory only allows us to listen to a part of the person rather than the whole person. I will then only discover what the theory tells me is there, and psychotherapy is not an intellectual search for what is already known. All theories are partial, but people are complex and whole. There are no isolated psychological problems. All problems are connected to each other as a total problem. Any presenting problem involves the whole person, and our wholeness cannot be analyzed, because as we take it apart we end up with pieces that cannot reflect the original whole. One can never fully understand a human being; there is always more going on than we are aware of.

I'd like to end with a little more Rumi, a quintessential non-dual poet:

> When the soul lies down in that grass
> the world is too full to talk about.
> Ideas, language, even the phrase,
> "each other" doesn't make any sense.[37]

NOTES

[1] Lao Tzu, *Tao Te Ching*, Chapter 56, trans. Stephen Adliss, Stanley Lombardo (Boston: Shambhala, 2007).

[2] Jalal al-Din Rumi, in Coleman Barks, ed., *The Essential Rumi*, trans. Coleman Barks and John Moyne (San Francisco: HarperSanFrancisco, 1994), p. 20.

[3] Rumi, in Maryam Mafi, ed. and trans., *Rumi: Hidden Music* (London: Thorsons, 2002).

[4] Rumi, in Coleman Barks, ed. and trans., *The Soul of Rumi, A New Collection of Ecstatic Poems* (San Francisco: HarperSanFrancisco, 2001), p. 196.

[5] See for example, George Kalamaras, *Reclaiming the Tacit Dimension: Symbolic Form in the Rhetoric of Silence* (Albany, NY: SUNY Press, 1994).

[6] C.G. Jung, *Letters, Vol. 2*, ed. Gerhard Adler, trans. R.F.C. Hull (Princeton: Princeton University Press, 1975), p. 363.

[7] 1 Kings 19:11-12, *The Holy Bible*, King James Version.

[8] Romans 8:26-27, *The Holy Bible*, New Revised Standard Version.

[9] Rainer Maria Rilke, *Letters to a Young Poet*, trans. Stephen Mitchell (NY: Random House, 1986), p. 4.

[10] T.S. Eliot, "Burnt Norton" [1936], in *Four Quartets* (Orlando: Harcourt, Inc., 1971), p. 19.

[11] Jiddu Krishnamurti, *This Light in Oneself: True Meditation* (Boston: Shambhala, 1999), p. 109.

[12] Meister Eckhart, in *Meditations on Nature, Meditations on Silence*, Roderick MacIver, ed. (North Ferrisburgh: Heron Dance Press, 2006), p. 61.

[13] Lao Tzu, Chapter 16, *Tao Te Ching*.

[14] Soren Kierkegaard, *Fear and Trembling*, trans. Alastair Hannay, reprinted (New York: Penguin Books, 2003).

[15] Leviticus 10:3, in *The Torah*, and in *The Holy Bible*, English Standard Version.

[16] Menachot 29b, *The Talmud*.

[17] Blaise Pascal, *Pensees* (New York: Penguin Classics, 1995), p. 66.

[18] C.G. Jung to Sigmund Freud, 6 January 1913, Letter 344J, *The Freud/Jung Letters*, ed. William McGuire, trans. Ralph Manheim and R.F.C. Hull, abridged ed. (Princeton, NJ: Prince University Press, 1994), p. 257.

[19] Sacha Emanuel Nacht, "Silence as an Integrative Factor," in *International Journal of Psychoanalysis, 45:1964*, pp. 299-303.

[20] Sigmund Freud, The Dynamics of Transference [1912], *Standard Edition of the Complete Psychological Works of Sigmund Freud (1911-1913)*, ed. James Strachey (London: Hogarth Press, 1962), Vol. 12, p. 101.

[21] Jacob Arlow, "Silence and the Theory of Technique," *Journal of the American Psychoanalytic Association,* 9:1961, pp. 44-55.

[22] Theodor Reik, "The Psychological Meaning of Silence," in *Psychoanalytic Review,* 55:1968, pp. 172-186.

[23] Ralph Greenson, "On the Silence and Sounds of the Analytic Hour," in *Journal of the American Psychoanalytic Association,* 9:1961, pp. 79-84.

[24] Nina Coltart, "The Silent Patient," in *Psychoanalytic Dialogues,* 4:1991, pp. 439-453.

[25] Emanuel Levinas, *Ethics and Infinity* (Pittsburgh: Duquesne University Press, 1985).

[26] Rumi, in Barks, *The Essential Rumi*, p. 32.

[27] Wayne B. Jonas and Cindy Crawford, "The Healing Presence: Can It be Reliably Measured?" in *Journal of Alternative and Complementary Medicine,* 10:2004, pp. 751-756.

[28] Shari M. Geller and Leslie S. Greenberg, "Therapeutic Presence: Therapists' Experience of Presence in the Psychotherapeutic Encounter," in *Person-Centered and Experiential Psychotherapies,* 1:2002, pp. 71-86.

[29] Orah T. Krug, "James Bugental and Irvin Yalom: Two Masters of Existential Therapy Cultivate Presence in the Therapeutic Encounter," in *Journal of Humanistic Psychology,* Vol. 49, no. 3, 2009, pp. 329-354.

[30] Geller and Greenberg, *Therapeutic Presence: A Mindful Approach to Effective Therapy* (Washington, D.C.: APA Press, 2011), p. 7.

[31] Daniel N. Stern, *The Present Moment in Psychotherapy and Everyday Life,* Norton Series on Interpersonal Neurobiology (New York: W.W. Norton & Co., 2004).

[32] *Ibid.,* p. 67.

[33] See for instance, Manuela Fleming, "Distinction Between Mental Pain and Psychic Suffering as Separate Entities in the Patient's Experience," in *International Forum of Psychoanalysis* (2006), pp. 195-201.

[34] Wilfred Bion, *Learning From Experience* (London: Karnac Books, 1984).

[35] Salman Akhtar, "Mental Pain and the Cultural Ointment of Poetry," in *International Journal of Psychoanalysis*: 2000, pp. 229-244.

[36] See, Krishnamurti, *Explorations into Insight* (London: Victor Gollancz, 1991).

[37] Rumi, in Barks, *The Essential Rumi,* p. 36.

2

An Exploration of Silence in Christian Mysticism
With the Desert Fathers, the Gospel of Thomas, and Meister Eckhart

Dariane Pictet

"But my words like silent raindrops fell / And
echoed / In the wells of silence . . ."[1]
—Simon and Garfunkel

Mysticism describes an experience that takes one beyond language, it is ineffable and is therefore essentially speechless. Its language is usually paradoxical, metaphorical and, at times, erotically charged as it attempts to describe the highest spiritual experience of union. Mysticism is often associated with the *via negativa*, the letting go of all images and words to describe god, the indescribable, whose name cannot be uttered. It engages with "unknowing" and experiences of the void, whether perceived as full or empty, or both. Meister Eckhart and St. John of the Cross are particularly well known western mystics who follow this approach. From the same period but emerging out of Anatolia, another voice,

Rumi, echoes, "The One is pure and silent. Why go on talking? The most radiant in me has never said a word."[2]

SILENCE AND THE DESERT

There was a tradition in early Christianity of retreating to the desert. In this unpeopled space, one comes face to face with oneself. Recently I was walking in the Sahara at sunset, musing on the silence that the desert fathers sought in the Sinai and Syria, where the first Christian monasteries were established. I became aware of a fear of what might lie beneath my feet; not a fear of the unknown, but of what I imagined could be there. My "preconception" took the shape of a snake, a lizard. Simultaneously, my eye surveyed the horizon, its vast expanses flooding me with feelings of freedom and openness. One part of me rejoiced, the other was full of preconceptions and fear. The oscillation between these two stances punctuate the individuation process, where moments of wholeness are followed by a more agitated sense of self.

The desert can evoke yellow dunes of golden sand, soft and welcoming, dissolving into cool nights where a navy sky is sprinkled by thousands of stars and we feel oneness with creation. Deserts can evoke a land of rough stones, of parched throats, loneliness, and overwhelming silence. Here, one can encounter our worst fears: devils in the night, temptation, complexes, at times a void of hope, of love, of relatedness, a loneliness "where silence like a cancer grows."[3] Jung begins his *Red Book* journey, "My soul leads me into the desert, into the desert of my own self. I did not think that my soul is a desert, a barren hot desert, dusty and without drink."[4]

The desert is like an embodied canvas where one paints and sees clearly the landscape of our interiority. The desert is where everything just is, and its silence mirrors psyche; at times nurturing, inspiring, exalted; at others, echoing arid meaninglessness. Deserts are also gateways to soft watery oases, where the source of life runs aplenty. Meister Eckhart sees the desert as a metaphor for a wilderness that we seek, for it is selfless and free. He refers to a "silent darkness into which no distinction or image ever peeped," the "trackless wasteland, the hidden desert" where even God "'unbecomes.'"[5] Timeless, and open, the desert describes a fluid state of consciousness, unattached to thinking and doing, where we stand in the present moment without obstacles between our being and truth. The mystical experience peaks in the ecstasy of standing outside duality, what some call eternity. One night, as I lay on the sands of the Sinai desert, my arms outstretched along the folds a dune, I felt a dizzying feeling that I could now die; it felt like both the beginning and the end of time and filled me an experience of pure being.

Let us note that Eckhart distinguishes god from the godhead, the latter being the unknowable transcendent mystery, just as Jung distinguishes god and the god image as describing two different realities. Jung is interested in describing the personal experience in the psyche, which is distinct from the "is-ness" of God, on which he cannot comment.

THE DESERT FATHERS

The Desert Fathers were men and women who lived in the desert of Egypt and founded monasteries beginning in the fourth century AD. We know about them from a collection of works called *The Sayings of the Desert Fathers*, out of which emerged the monastic tradition of Eastern Orthodoxy, such as the one still practiced on Mount Athos.[6] There, the tradition of Hesychasm, of retiring inward to experience God, is still practiced today; *hesychia* is Greek for stillness, quiet. In the first half of the fifth century the hesychast Abraham of Nathpar wrote, "There is a silence of the tongue, there is a silence of the whole body, there is the silence of the soul, there is the silence of the mind, and there is the silence of the spirit."[7]

St. Gregory Palamas, who spent most of his life on Mt. Athos in the thirteenth century, described Hesychasm as a way of life in which the adept seeks inner silence and the cleansing of passions that may, through grace, lead to mystical union.[8] With vigilant sobriety the hesychast tries to avoid "thieves," the tempting thoughts that lead to sin. His intention is to experience a way of being that is free of images, called the "guard of the mind." Only then can the adept partake of the silence of God and speak the Jesus prayer from the heart. A longing for God becomes perceptible through these ascetic practices that essentially attempt to turn the adept away from cluttering thoughts into spiritual contemplation. When the body is quiet, the restless mind is quiet, the yearnings of soul and feeling are quiet, the stirrings of vision and spirituality are quiet, in this silence communion is possible. Father Seraphim—who lives presently on Mt. Athos (and whom I will never meet, as the island is forbidden to women)—teaches the practice of inner silence, of entering a vast spaciousness, away from the senses. He describes the following practices: to meditate like a mountain, like a red poppy, like an ocean, like a bird.

To "meditate like a mountain" emphasizes firstly the body: to hold oneself in a straight posture and to learn to be still, stable, solid as a rock, and to experience that "mountains know another time, another rhythm."[9] Here one enters a boundless present. After this experience of eternity, paradoxically, the next meditation teaches the transiency of life. To meditate like a red poppy is to discover orientation, to "turn from the depth of [one's self] towards the light."[10] The teaching lies in humility (*humus* in Latin, meaning ground) and contemplation of the cycles of life—the tenderness, fragility, and evanescence of flowers that grow, blossom, whither, and die.

After acquiring right posture and attitude, one learns to meditate like an ocean. Observing the ebb and flow of breath, one notices the thoughts that come and go on the surface of the ocean, while in the depths, all is quiet. To pray is first of all to breathe; and the breath is pneuma, taking in the presence of God. Conscious breathing reveals a pulsation that takes us from oneness to duality and back, integrating both fields of experience. To meditate like a bird is "to breathe while singing," to find the spontaneous hum that rises up when we are happy and fills us with a song of praise for the beauty of creation.[11] Like an eastern mantra, this vibration on the breath leads to inner silence. Meditation comes from the Greek *melete / meletan*, which was translated in Latin as *meditari / meditatio*, and its root means "to murmur in whisper."

After these forays into the mineral, vegetal, and animal worlds, the last two meditations in this hesychastic practice focus on the next stage of development: that of human beings, who have lost Eden and a natural relationship with the world. Man, who has the gift of reflection, can open himself to compassion. To meditate like Abraham "frees the heart of its obsessive need to judge and condemn . . ."[12] It means also the ability to sacrifice our highest values, to "make sacred" our surrender to the will of God, just as Abraham who sacrificed his son. Lastly, to meditate like Jesus, the boundless one, perfects all the previous practices and the overflow of selfless love streaming down from the Father is felt within the intimacy of one's heart.

THE GOSPEL OF THOMAS

I now turn to Jesus, who called himself the Son of Man, and announced an inner kingdom, accessible to all, here and now. His teachings were compiled in *The Gospel of Thomas*, which was found in Nag Hammadi, in the Egyptian desert in 1945. The author, Thomas Didymus, is the disciple who is said to have travelled to South India as early as AD 52, who died in Madras, and whom some speculate to have been the twin brother of Jesus Christ of Nazareth ("didymus," in Greek, meaning twin). The Nag Hammadi coptic papyrus dates back to circa 350-400 AD, but lay untouched in a cave for almost two millennia. The original gospel in Greek or Aramaic may even anti-date the canonical gospels of the New Testament; they are, it seems, "as early as, or earlier, than Mark, Matthew, Luke and John."[13]

Here we are in the presence of a personal encounter with the divine, as witnessed by the Apostle Thomas. Unlike the canonical gospels, this apocryphal text has not undergone centuries of revision and re-translation. The words of Jesus, pristinely enclosed in the earthen jars surrounded by desert sands, were suddenly revealed to us, fresh and seemingly unedited, in simple statements called *logions*. The Gnostic gospels found at Nag Hammadi include what is now called the Jung Codex, a set of manuscripts purchased by the Jung Foundation of Zürich, as they were of considerable interest for their depiction of the internal quality of religious experience: "'. . . it is from this ground of inner silence, rather than from mental agitation, that these words of Yeshua [Jesus][14] can bear their fruit of Light.'"[15]

The Gospel of Thomas appears to lay down the unadorned words of the one who was later to become Christ. "Christos," meaning the anointed, sanctified one, is a Greek translation of the Hebrew word for messiah, and is linked to the prophetic tradition that focuses on the historical Jesus and is assimilated to the doctrines of resurrection and virgin birth. Unburdened by canon and theology, the Gospel of Thomas focuses on the immanence of the kingdom preached by Jesus: "His disciples said to him, 'Twenty-four prophets have spoken in Israel, and they all spoke of you.' He said to them, 'You have disregarded the Living One who is in your presence, and you have spoken of the dead.'"[16] This emphasis on the living presence throws one directly back to oneself. Jesus then, is the teacher through whom we can awaken to a state of living presence:

> Yeshua said:
> Whoever drinks from my mouth
> will become like me,
> and I will become them,
> and what was hidden from them will be revealed.[17]

Unlike the canonical Jesus who comes as Savior, the redeemer of sins, this "living Jesus" offers guidance to the spiritual seeker, who can potentially become identical to him. He calls us to understand that our attitude to inwardness can determine our fate:

> Yeshua said:
> When you bring forth *that* within you,
> then *that* will save you.
> If you do not, then *that* will kill you.[18]

We have the capacity for light and liberation as well as the ability to be self-destructive. But what is *that* which can either save us or destroy us? Is it the *living presence* cited above, is it love, is it self-knowledge? "Jesus says: 'Whoever knows all, if he is lacking one thing, he is (already) lacking everything.'"[19] What is this elusive unnamable quality that makes all the difference? If it is love, why isn't stated? Perhaps because this points to this ineffable something, which is perhaps no thing that can make us or unmake us, but can set us on a quest that will be utterly transformative. The tools of this seeking are wonder and opening to the presence of All, the essence at the core of being.

The emphasis on the internal experience continues in the following logion:

> Yeshua said:
> Why do you wash the outside of the cup?
> Do you not understand
> that the one who made the outside
> also made the inside?[20]

The empty space that makes up the inside of the cup is the silence out of which the logos first appeared, but this appearance of duality should not distract us from the source. Yeshua said: "When you make the two into One, you will be the Son of Man."[21] The Son of Man inhabits both fields of time: the eternal one, as that which brought bliss to my desert experience, and historical time, in which our personal biography and identity are embedded. In Jung's view, the reconciliation of such dualities, including the conscious and unconscious attitudes, is part of the individuation process—itself arising from a wider consciousness called the Self.

Jesus encourages us to develop insight while we are on this plane of existence, in the here and now, not after death: "What you are waiting for has already come, but you do not see it."[22] Blinded by our projections, we do not see reality clearly. He even goes further in telling us that what is not accomplished here will not be accessible there:

> Yeshua said:
> Look to the Living One while you are alive.
> If you wait until you are dead,
> you will search in vain for the vision.[23]

This deadness can refer to the state after existence or to a state of inner inertness, devoid of light, wonder, and attunement to the spirit that shines through everything.

There is something vital that we need to bring forth, to know, to encounter, while we are in this difficult, at times unsatisfying existence. Another reality stands in front of our eyes, and we need to make it transparent, or make ourselves transparent to transcendence, as Joseph Campbell might say. Yeshua said:

> The kingdom of the Father
> is spread out over the whole earth,
> and people do not see it.[24]

Surely this kingdom is not a place, but refers to an inner state of being that is available and to which we need to awaken.

We mustn't get too attached to the landscapes of mind and stone that we encounter in our journey through life. "Jesus says: Become passers-by," emphasizing that we are transient passengers.[25] Non–attachment, simplicity, and the openness of the child are the companions of the spiritual traveler. "Blessed are the solitary and elect, for you will find the kingdom. For you are from it, and to it you will return."[26]

Arguably, Jung's *Red Book* could be likened to a Gnostic gospel as it describes the redemption of Jung's soul, lost to him in the inner depths, then gradually awakening and ascending to consciousness as a trusted and valued inner partner. Solitariness is not only solitude of place but also a solitude of being, a silence of the mind, of expectations and preconceptions, a return to the boundless, undifferentiated source.

MEISTER ECKHARDT

Meister Eckhart, a thirteenth-century Dominican friar, wrote his sermons on spiritual transformation. Eckhart's first sermon begins,

> For a while all things were wrapped in peaceful silence and night was in the middle of its swift course . . . then a secret word leaped out down from heaven, out of the royal throne, to me.[27]

Eckhart's peaceful silence precedes all creation; out of this "womb" emerges the word that sets the conceptual world into being. Silence is at the origin of everything; from it all of creation unfolds. He adds, "The Heavenly father utters a word and utters it eternally . . . To hear it, all voices and sounds must die away and there must be pure quiet—perfect stillness."[28]

This "word," being uttered eternally, resonating in us and around us, is like the echo of the Big Bang, which is apparently audible on a particular wavelength. For Eckhart, silence not only precedes sound and human chatter—silence is also an absence of presumption.[29] The poem below, "Granum Sinapsis" ("A Grain of the Mustard Seed of the Most Beautiful Divinity") is usually attributed to Meister Eckhart:

> . . .
> The way leads you
> into a wondrous desert
> which extends wide
> and immeasurably far.
> The desert knows
> neither time nor space.
> Its nature is unique.
>
> Never has a foot
> crossed the domain of the desert,
> created reason
> has never attained it.
> It is, and yet no one knows what.
> It is here, there,
> far, near,
> deep, high,

so that
it is neither the one nor the other.

Light, clear,
completely dark,
nameless,
unknown,
without beginning and also without end,
it rests in itself,
unveiled, without disguise.
Who knows what its dwelling is?
Let him come forth
and tell us of what shape it is.[30]

Eckhart describes a state of consciousness that is virginal, "free of all alien images," a state of openness and complete receptivity. A state that he calls "the Virgin"—being not bound to the results of actions, but free of the past and the future, empty of preconceptions, unpenetrated, whole-in-one.

According to Meister Eckhart, when a man "conceives God in himself" he is a virgin, but when "God . . . become[s] fruitful in him" he is a wife.[31] The soul is infused with the spirit, and in her delight and gratitude, she conceives, creates, enables. Only then do we stand in the silence of Being and conceive God; the feeling of oneness becomes generative. It is not just a passive basking in eternal bliss but it adds a dimension of activity, of creativity, to the human experience. This is the metaphor illustrated in the Bible by Mary, the pregnant virgin, who is both maidenly and mother. Mary, in the Annunciation answers, "Let it be" to the mystery presented to her by the Angel informing her that she is to be both virgin and mother and conceive of the holy spirit. The latter is a manifestation of the unknown, without which nothing new is ever conceived.

"A virgin who is a wife is free and unpledged, without attachment; she is always equally close to God and to herself."[32] *From that ground, she fruitfully bears with God* an abundance—an abundance which Eckhart sees as emanating from that same ground of silence out of which God utters the eternal word. Is this *word* that emerges out of *perfect stillness,* that *word* which all voices and sounds must die away to hear, the same that Thomas describes as *that* which can save us or destroy us, a *living presence* that must be born is us? Is this a presence that is both formless and creative?

Bede Griffiths, a Benedictine monk who settled in Bangalore in the 1950's, has been called the "equivalent to the Hesychast," one who goes beyond silence to stillness of heart. He saw the contemplative process not only as one of transcendence but also as a painful experience of self-discovery: "Above all we have to go beyond words and images and concepts. No imaginative vision or conceptual framework is adequate to the great reality."[33]

SILENCE IN ANALYSIS

In analysis and psychotherapy, silence can be welcoming when it suspends judgments and assumptions. When we listen actively, we offer a clear expanse of time, an open horizon, in which the anaylsand can dwell and feel received and accepted. As Eckhart says, "It is in the stillness, in the silence that the word of god is to be heard."[34] Similarly, Jung offers, "Solitude is a fount of healing which makes my life worth living. Talking is often a torment for me, and I need many days of silence to recover from the futility of words."[35] The inner voice that rises up from the Self offers a perspective that emerges from the spirit of the depth, not the spirit of the time.

Based as it is on verbal exchange, then, is the "talking cure" futile? Or is it the pause, the breath between the words that offers healing and insight? An analyst's "hovering attention" enables his or her opening to that which emerges spontaneously from within the mutual field—including silence, with the experience of being in an unformulated, imaginal depth, a ground out of which assumptions emerge. In the *Red Book*, Jung describes this as an experience of "forethinking," or being in a diffuse awareness that precedes form and language.

"Jesus said, '. . . no physician heals those who know him.'"[36] To "know" someone is to frame them with our assumptions, thus to limit him or her with our subjectivity. What we think we know about the other often comes out of our own projections and we end up seeing ourselves, not the other person. To start with the assumption that an "other" is ultimately unknowable allows us to widen our perceptions and let in what is hidden from view.

Similarly, what our analysands personally know or believe to know about us can inhibit the healing process as they cannot freely project on us their own views and attitudes. Thus, as analysts we hope to offer ourselves, silently, as a canvas—like that "canvas" of the desert—onto which our analysands can see their preconceptions and unconscious contents emerge and, hopefully, be integrated in consciousness.

Ultimately, just as the godhead cannot be known, so do we remain partly incomprehensible to one another and even to ourselves. For example, an analysand might say that his mother was always a tender, facilitating loving person—yet he repeatedly reports encounters with dark and difficult women who criticize him endlessly. I myself, in my analytical chair, might also feel criticized and demeaned. Then, I will have to wonder if the analysand has idealized his mother, has not yet humanized his mother complex by becoming aware of his mother's shadow aspects, which might have been wounding to him. Until they become more fully conscious, these shadow aspects will continually be met in the outer world to help the person enlarge his understanding of woman, of mother, of the conflicting nature of reality. Transference feelings are eventually replaced by imagination, as we revisit the life story; we move from what is unconsciously known, mother's shadow, to a re-imagining of mother that includes the unknowable aspects of mother, of self, of existence.

Jung's understanding was that we do not cure neuroses, we outgrow them by making the suffering of the conflict conscious. Jung also postulated that there is a mysterious point where psyche and body are one, and out of this point healing symbols emerge and make transformation possible. Jung calls this psychoid archetype the anima mundi. Eckhart also refers to the essence of soul that precedes image formation:

> The central silence is the purest element of the soul, the soul's most exalted place, the core, the essence of the soul. It is there, where no creature may enter, nor any idea, and therefore the soul neither thinks nor acts, not entertains any idea, either of itself or of anything else.[37]

So, we gather that it is not intellectual knowledge that heals but gnosis, a deeper knowing, which includes a relationship to alterity, or otherness. This otherness, or third dimension, enters and transforms the relational field through imagination. In Jungian terms this would be an aspect of the transcendent function, itself understood to unite opposites by constellating a symbol that reframes polarities in a new, non-deadlocked context.

The transcendent function may be experienced among other ways through active imagination, a creative activity that explores the imagery of dreams, sandplay, drawing, or even dancing. The emerging symbols can heal the split between the conscious and the unconscious attitude by creating a new middle ground that was previously invisible to consciousness. As in Eckhart's vision, "'When the soul wishes to experience something, she throws an image of the experience before her and enters into her own image.'"[38] Active imagination, exemplified by the *Red Book*, is less characterized by a willful or conscious dwelling on images than by a reaching into the imaginal sphere, where the unknown takes shape and visits us in the form of autonomous, often surprising symbols. Freed from ideas of right and wrong, we accept the symbol, allowing its energy transform our conscious attitude.

* * * *

There is something about the desert that describes existence in its simplest form; walking through it, we become attentive to all shifts of movement, color, and signs of organic life. In the same way, silence is the ground on which sound and ideas become manifest. Out of this void of form, this *via negativa*, we return to the ontological origin, to the very ground of being. This perhaps is what is meant in Jesus' words, "Blessed are you, the poor, for yours is the Kingdom of Heaven."[39]

Emptiness and fullness alternate as our consciousness expands and retracts, oscillating between timelessness and time bound experiences. Thus, as Eckhart conveys, "A hand in my soul can reach out and touch Jerusalem / as my other hand tastes the beauty of the Rhine."[40] On one hand, I breathe in the boundless eternal freedom of the desert, on the other hand I taste mortality, fear, and finitude—and the fluctuation between these two fields lend dignity and purpose to existence.

And the rest is silence...

NOTES

[1] Paul Simon and Art Garfunkel, "Sounds of Silence" [1964], Track 1, *The Sounds of Silence*, producer Bob Johnston, recorded at CBS

Studios, Nashville, 1966. Lyrics at http://www.lyricsdepot.com/simon-garfunkel/sounds-of-silence.html, accessed April 17, 2013.

[2] Rumi, in Coleman Barks, ed. and trans., *The Soul of Rumi: A New Collection of Ecstatic Poems* (San Francisco: Harper, 2001), p. 196.

[3] Simon and Garfunkel, "Sounds of Silence."

[4] C.G. Jung, *The Red Book: Liber Novus, A Reader's Edition*, Sonu Shamdasani, ed. and trans., trans. John Peck, Mark Kyburz (New York: W.W. Norton & Company, 2009), p. 141.

[5] Meister Eckhart, in Edmund Colledge and Bernard McGinn, trans., *Meister Eckhart, The Essential Sermons, Commentaries, Treatises and Defense* (New York: Paulist Press, 1981), p. 204.

[6] See for example, Benedicta Ward, trans., *The Sayings of the Desert Fathers: The Apopthegmata Patrum: The Alphabetic Collection*, Cistercian Studies, Book 59, Rev. Ed. (Collegeville, MN: Cistercian Publications, 1975).

[7] Abraham of Nathpar, in Sebastian Brock, trans., *The Syriac Fathers on Prayer and the Spiritual Life*, Vol. 101 (Collegeville, MN: Cistercian Publications 1987), p. 189.

[8] Gregory Palamas, *Defence des Saints Hesychastes,* ed. Jean Meyendorff (Louvain: Spicilegium Sacrum Lovaniese, 1973), pp. 2, 21, 14.

[9] Father Seraphim, in Jean-Yves Leloup, *Being Still: Reflections on an Ancient Mystical Tradition*, trans. Martin S. Laird (New York: Paulist Press, 2003), p. 3.

[10] *Ibid.,* in Leloup, *Being Still,* p. 4.

[11] *Ibid.,* p. 7.

[12] *Ibid.,* p. 9.

[13] Elaine Pagels, *The Gnostic Gospels* (London: Weidenfeld & Nicholson, 1980), p. xvii.

[14] My use of "Yeshua" or "Jesus" corresponds respectively with the cited sources.

[15] Jean-Yves Leloup, quoted by Jacob Needleman, in "Introduction," in Leloup, *The Gospel of Thomas: The Gnostic Wisdom of Jesus*, trans. Joseph Rowe (Rochester, NY: Inner Traditions, 2005), p. xi.

[16] Leloup, *The Gospel of Thomas*, Logion 52, p. 31.

[17] "The Text of the Gospel of Thomas," Logion 108, in Leloup, *The Gospel,* p. 55.

[18] Logion 70, in Leloup, *The Gospel*, p. 41, original italics.

[19] "The Gospel of Thomas," Logion 67, in Patterson and Robinson.

[20] "The Text of the Gospel of Thomas," Logion 89, in Leloup, *The Gospel*, p. 47.

[21] Logion 106, in Leloup, *The Gospel*, p. 55.

[22] *Ibid.*

[23] Logion 51, in Leloup, *The Gospel*, p. 31.

[24] Logion 59, in Leloup, *The Gospel*, p. 35.

[25] Logion 113, in Leloup, *The Gospel*, p. 57.

[26] "The Gospel of Thomas," Logion 42, in Patterson and Robinson.

[27] *Ibid.*, Logion 49, in Patterson and Robinson.

[28] Meister Eckhart, *Meister Eckhart: A Modern Translation*, trans. Raymond B. Blakney (New York: Harper Torchbooks, 1941), p. 95.

[29] *Ibid.*, *Meister Eckhart*, trans. Blakney, p. 242.

[30] Eckhart, in Colledge and McGinn, *Meister Eckhart: the Essential*, p. 49.

[31] Anonymous [Eckhart], "Granum Sinapis" [ca. 1300], in Karen J. Campbell, ed., *German Mystical Writings: Hildegard of Bingen, Meister Eckhart, Jacob Boehme, and Others* (New York: Continuum, 2002), p. 143, © Karen J. Campbell, reprinted by permission of Bloomsbury Publishing, Plc. Author's note: Campbell and others attribute the poem variously to "Anonymous" or to an author in "Eckhart's circle." Other scholars argue there is no evidence that conclusively excludes Eckhart's authorship; see for example Kurt Ruh, "Granum sinapis," 2010 [untitled website in German], at http://www.eckhart.de/index.htm?granum.htm (accessed 12 February, 2014).

[32] Eckhart, *Meister Eckhart*, trans. Blakney, p. 178.

[33] Eckhart, in Colledge and McGinn, *Meister Eckhart: The Essential*, p. 178.

[34] Bede Griffiths, *Essential Writings*, ed. Thomas Matus, Modern Spiritual Masters Series (New York: Orbis Books, 2004).

[35] Eckhart, *Meister Eckhart*, trans. Blakney, p. 107.

[36] C.G. Jung to Gustave Schmaltz, 30 May 1957, in *C.G. Jung Letters Vol. 2: 1951 to 1961*, ed. Gerhard Adler, trans. R.F.C. Hull (London: Routledge, 1975), p. 363.

[37] "The Gospel of Thomas (II, 2)," trans. Thomas O. Lambdin, Logion 31, in James M. Robinson, ed., *The Nag Hammadi Library in English: The Definitive New Translation of the Gnostic Scriptures, Complete in One Volume,* Rev. Ed. (San Francisco: Harper Collins, 1990), p.130.

[38] Eckhart, *Meister Eckhart,* trans. Blakney, p. 96.

[39] Eckhart, in David Gordon, *Mindful Dreaming: A Practical Guide for Emotional Healing Through Transformative Mythic Journeys* (Franklin Lakes, NJ: Career Press, 2007), p. 47.

[40] "The Text of the Gospel of Thomas," Logion 54, in Leloup, *The Gospel,* p. 33.

[41] Eckhart, "Jerusalem," in Daniel Ladinsky, trans., *Love Poems from God: Twelve Sacred Voices from the East and West* (New York: Penguin, 2002), p. 96.

3

THE SILENCE OF "GOD"

Bernard Sartorius

The forthcoming discussion could begin in a preacher's mode, asserting that god has become silent in our time; that our civilization has therefore become meaninglessness except for a dumb and numb consumerism; that god is most loudly mentioned by fanatical fundamentalists, if not by terrorists. I could look backward to those blessed times when god spoke through Jesus Christ to Christians, through the Prophet Mohammed to Muslims, or through dreams and the unconscious to Jungians. I could follow our colleague Wolfgang Giegerich, who asserts in his recent works that even C.G. Jung's "gods"—the archetypal voices within us—tend today to become meaningless.[1] However I will take a different tact, neither assuming that god's silence means absence—nor even assuming that god *ought* to be heard. I understand "god" here phenomenologically as that which "inspires" us and lends meaning to our existence.

Let's briefly consider some experiences of silence: the silence of an empty house; or differently, the silence of a house when the people living in it have moved out, or passed away; the silence of a person who has no answer or withholds an answer; the silence in the moments before an answer comes; the silence in the still of a desert or a mountain top; the all-filling, massive silence of a corpse; the vibrating silence of the stars in the night sky; the silence in the interlude between two movements of a piece of music; the silence in the aftermath of an explosion; the classroom hushed by the teacher's command of silence; the silence at high noon, in front of the saloon, before the shooting starts; the space encompassing an old couple no longer in need of words to communicate their love; the space encompassing another old couple, no longer having anything to share; the silence of the meditating monk; the silence of a stone, a flower. Such scenarios contain a wide range of very different psychic situations that variously signify relatedness, contentment, a radical absence, a void. So we see that if "god" is conceived as that which inspires meaning, the preacher's understanding of an audible god inadequately circumscribes reality. The manifold experiences of silence dissolve the either/or dilemma, god either speaks or is silent and absent.

There could be another possibility, one that includes the symbolism of "god" but is less burdened by the expectation that meaningful messages emanate from a source far away from the ego, such as from a life-transcendent being or from deep within the unconscious or the Self. This kind of hermeneutics—one which reaches beyond the question, "is god silent or not?"—finds expression in symbolic material from non-European cultures, especially the Asian, that value the experience of non-duality. However here I want to refer to the familiar European Grimm's fairy tales, in particular, "The Blue Light."[2] The tale's central symbol, an ever-burning blue light, alludes to something beyond, or at least complementary to, the dualistic questions as to whether a god from "above" is silent or not, whether deep in the unconscious a Self speaks or not. The title alone is already revealing: whereas "light" symbolically arouses the idea of consciousness as such, the color blue can point to the archetype of the spirit. But in its farthest reaches—as in the sky or the sea—luminous blue turns utterly black. Thus, being at once *luminous* and *blue/dark*, the light of the fairy tale infers a holistic quality of consciousness that integrates opposites—the light and dark, the conscious and unconscious, and hence others like the meaningful and absurd, the silent and not silent god. A radical paradox, the luminous-and-dark-light could stand as the image of a non-dualistic hermeneutics that opens to the reality of *existence*, to being alive in the here and now, free of projections that harbor illusions of meanings beyond. In other words, a blue/black light could refer to a consciousness that need not seek meaning outside itself. And as we see in the tale, this blue light "never goes out." Thus we have a symbol of an *ever-present psychic potential and vector*, as opposed to an empirical psychological condition that can be concretely attained.

"The Blue Light" tells the story of a soldier who, because of his many wounds, was dismissed without pension after many years of faithful service in the King's army. "I need you no longer," the King told him, "and you will not receive any more money for only he receives wages who renders me service...." The story continues, in summary:

> As the soldier wanders aimlessly in the forest, unemployed and starving, he happens upon a witch's house. "I will be compassionate," she says, "and take you in if you will do what I wish." So the soldier has to "dig all around [her] garden," and "chop a load of wood, and chop it small." One day, she commands him to retrieve from an old dried-up well her "light which burns blue, and never goes out." She lowers him down the well in a basket, and he retrieves the light—but realizing her "evil intention," he refuses to hand it over until his feet are on the ground. Infuriated, the witch drops him back into the well, he clutching the blue light as he falls. But he is unable get out by himself and the witch of course does not help. Sitting for a long time at the bottom, in despair and on the brink of death, he happens to find his tobacco pipe. "This will be my last pleasure," he thinks to himself, and uses the blue light to spark his pipe. Suddenly a little black man appears, offering help. The little man leads him out of the well, allowing him on the way to take the witch's hidden treasures. Fulfilling the soldier's next wish, the little man binds up the witch and takes her to the judge, who orders her hung on the gallows. The man promises to be at the soldier's command whenever he lights up his pipe with the blue light. So with his help the soldier avenges the King's heartlessness by abducting his daughter, the princess. The soldier forces her to work at night as his maidservant, and each morning when the cock crows the little black man takes her back to her own bed. After several nights, the king discovers where his daughter had been toiling each night, and persuades the judge to condemn the soldier to death although he had "done

nothing wicked." On the way to the gallows, the solider asks the King to let him have one last smoke. At once the little black man appears, rescues the soldier, and bludgeons down the King and all the false judges. In the end the king begs for mercy, and gives the soldier his kingdom and his daughter to wed as wife.[3]

The witch is often said to be an image of the dark side of the mother archetype, an archetype which itself can stand for reality as such and the origin of all "good" and "evil." The witch's possession of the blue light at the tale's outset thus immediately points to an aspect of the meaning embraced in a non-dualistic hermeneutics: Psychic movement is induced by real life experience, including not only the so-called "good," but also suffering and the anticipation of death. This "blue light effect," as we might call it, seems to be mirrored in the fairy tale's soldier: Embattled, injured, and dismissed from the King's service, he could personify an ego wounded and rejected by a "kingly" consciousness, that is, a dualistic mindset that frames life in clear-cut values—for instance, ranking efficiency against inefficiency, as is so typical in today's collective.

When psychic conditions are shifting, we often feel ourselves to be "in the woods," "in the dark," helpless, homeless, debased, and starving. In such a state the soldier stumbles one night upon the house of the witch, who takes him into her service. Gardening and chopping wood for the witch, he is far removed from army life, when he fought visible enemies and consciously tackled difficult circumstances. His lowly work for the witch could be an image of the loss of the dominant "kingly" value system—and at the same time, a metaphor for the arduous effort needed to survive such loss. Under such circumstances, to merely survive is to do a good job. But underlying this constellation—a sterile one, according to extraverted criteria—the blue light burns, meaning that in the holistic perspective, such basic experience also counts, holds objective value.

We soon learn that the blue light has fallen into the waterless well, and the witch sends the soldier to retrieve it. But when he emerges, she drops him back into the pit—the blue light going down with him. The tale as such suggests that continuous movement away from a dualistic consciousness involves precisely such feelings as betrayal, despair, and hopelessness, among others. Descent into depression, the fear of death, and other abysmal experiences seem to reflect the aim of the blue light vector to dissolve our fixation on luminous musings about god. Belonging to the constellation as well is the background of the soldier's battle days and injuries, implying a loss of childish naiveté, which we imagine to endow him with the cunning to hold on the blue light as he falls. So here again we see symbolically a situation in which a tough life and woundedness foster the transformation of consciousness.

Sitting at the bottom of the well, resolved to imminent death, the soldier treats himself to a last smoke, starting up his pipe with the blue light. As we know from many contexts—the cultural and personal—pipe smoking can be a ritual act of letting go, a seeking of release from an either/or orientation. Popping up in this moment of conjunction between ego-directed activity and release, the "little black man" personifies the completely unexpected possibility of a different outlook, and would seem to illustrate what Jung calls the "mercurial" nature of the psyche. In other words, the emergence of a really new quality of consciousness can transpire through synchronicity, when an unanticipated symbolic constellation appears, materializing with no causal relationship to foregoing events (here, a wounding of the ego and a yielding to despair and the prospect of death). It is as if to say, in the moment of surrender to the worst imaginable fate, the ever-present blue light "kindles" a shift of mind, which opens access to valuable psychic energies. There is no need for reference to a fantasy of "god" or any other meaning, although the ego may well desire it.

The transformation of consciousness takes place in the well, in the here and now of the deepest psychic pit. This situation gives access to the witch's hidden treasures; that is, deep psychic energies become available when one surrenders the claim to know for sure where to go, which god's voice to follow, or when one wearies of despairing about "god's silence." As the witch soon hangs from the gallows, we sense that as consciousness gradually becomes less dualistic, a deadly fate is "suspended." The ability to accept suffering grows, and death is a wee, wee bit less feared.

Avenging his harsh and unjust treatment, the soldier next commands the little black man to abduct the King's daughter, who is then forced to nocturnal servitude. The princess of fairy tale—symbolically, the anima—is usually obtained only with difficulty, often only by seemingly unjust or vengeful ways. This motif, and that of the princess's own lowly labor, point to a hard advent of the feminine and obstacles that can lie in the path to the integration of the erotic in the sense of authentic relatedness to oneself, to others, and to reality. We now can see now why the query into god's silence, if pressed, could become a pitfall. It could introduce the quest for an outside reference, the quest for an external god or meaning—especially connected for instance with questions like one that surely now lurks in the backs of our minds: "How can one justify getting in touch with the feminine by abducting and subjecting it to slave labor?" The answer would be: underlying these activities, like all others in this tale, is the blue light, which, psychologically speaking, aims to contain the tension of opposites. Here the feminine comes to hold diurnal and nocturnal qualities—for the princess, previously being "nothing but" the royal father's darling, now holds this position by day *and* labors at night for the wounded and debased soldier. Holding such oppositional tension in reality, consciousness tends to empty itself of idealistic expectations—as here, the inference that relatedness to the feminine should develop according to some ideal or notion of fairness.

In the soldier's capture and death sentence we have an illustration of the psyche's tendency to repeatedly regress to a previous quality of consciousness, to old references and reflexes. According to the meaning of the underlying blue light, regressive constellations—so-called pathological moments—hold their own objective value in a life lived in the here and now. The soldier is delivered again, this time from the gallows, by using the blue light to stoke up his pipe. As we see again, the possibility of release from a "kingly," dualistic hermeneutics can be constellated by a paradoxical conjunction, namely that of ego-activity joined with the objective potential of a non-dualistic openness to the unknown. Similarly, the marriage of the soldier and princess, with his ascent as the new King, follows the tale's dynamism toward a gradual change in the mode of seeing and perceiving, a change of "hermeneutical spectacles."

From beginning to end, the tale depicts one rough scene after another—from the soldier's cruel discharge, all the way through to the solid thrashing of the King and his henchmen. The blue light is present all along, from the time it is in the witch's possession, until it helps the soldier's escape from the gallows. The psyche's movement is this archetypal opening to lightness *and* darkness, to god speaking *and* not speaking, to meaning *and* meaninglessness. There is not one single episode—even the most desperate or regressive—that doesn't somehow foster this potential quality of consciousness. Accompanied always by the blue light, every constellation and moment in our lives leads, eases us psychically beyond our present frame.

We have seen in this fairy tale and its central motif—the ever-burning blue light—an archetypal impulse of the collective unconscious to dissolve the dualistic dilemma. This archetype moves us toward recognition of the objective value of every life moment, be it light or dark, be it filled with meaning or god's audible voice, or not. Whether it is the ego or some other part of the psyche that avails itself of the blue light, it is always present, making every second in life indispensable for soul-making. In practice this means that we embrace each person's biography as being *the* valid way, however blessed, joyful, dull, or painful it may be. The blue light is the archetypal image of our ever-present and enduring potential to accept our lives, and every moment in them, as the one and only reality. In the fairy tale the blue light belongs neither to the witch, nor to the soldier, nor to the little black man, but lies behind all of them and all episodes. In other words, the potential for holistic consciousness cannot be identified with any particular frame of mind or individual—as some false gurus or their followers tend to pretend. Nor is there a particular psychic constellation that would be more "blue-lightish" than others. High levels of activity are included, for the blue light just as much accompanies the soldier's ascent to the throne, by which we understand a position from which one's life is actively and consciously managed.

By now the relevance of "god's silence" seems to have vanished to the point of becoming silent itself. Beyond the projection on a god far outside or a Self far inside, one can ask if the "real" issue would be that of our silence or non-silence in relationship to our own lives. The hermeneutics symbolized by the blue light opens questions about our sometimes wordy reactions to the mystery of being alive in the here and now. What and how much do I have to say about this reality? How honestly do I speak? Can I remain silent?

The novel, *Nausea*, by the French author and philosopher Jean-Paul Sartre, portrays a conflict between the protagonist Antoine and a nameless but very loquacious "self taught man" (*l'Autodidacte*), the personification of Antoine's alter ego.[4] And so we find Antoine, the unemployed and dejected writer, struggling with the self taught man, who bursts with scientific, philosophical, and psychological explanations about everything conceivable. Only when Antoine discovers the reality of his *existence* and everything around him, does he realize that he himself can be silent. And out of this silence *might* emerge a few true words that express the experience of simply existing:

> A gas lamp glowed, I thought the lamp lighter had already passed. The children watch for him because he gives the signal for them to go home. But it was only a last ray of the setting sun. The sky was still clear, but the earth was bathed in shadow. The crowd was dispersing, you distinctly heard the [sighing] of the sea. A young woman, leaning with both hands on the balustrade, lifted her blue face towards the sky, barred in black by lipstick. For a moment I wondered if I were not going to love humanity. But after all, it was their Sunday, not mine.
>
> The first light to go on was that of the lighthouse on the Ile Caillebotte. A little boy stopped near me and murmured in ecstasy, "Oh! The lighthouse!"
>
> Then I felt my heart swell with a great feeling of adventure.[5]

This mode of being intensifies, bringing Antoine ever closer to a "blue light" experience, toward accepting the here and now:

> I *was* the root of the chestnut tree. Or rather I was entirely conscious of its existence. . . . Time had stopped: a small black pool at my feet; it was impossible for anything to come *after* that moment.[6]

Such rare, experienced immediacy of being dissolves our attachment to those noisy causalities and hopes that otherwise bind us to the past and the future. Here, too, Sartre illuminates another, essential aspect of the blue light effect: an evocation of silence and an honesty and simplicity of mind, which preclude compensatory talk (including debate about god's silence or non-silence). As with the boy's ecstatic murmur, "Oh the lighthouse," the truth and depth of an archetypal "blue light" moment finds expression in very few words.

To review, the blue light in our fairy tale can be seen as an archetypal image of enduring psychic movement toward non-dualistic consciousness, a way of perceiving that avoids the trap of dilemmas such as god is either silent or not; the psyche is either pathological or healthy; life is either meaningful or absurd; perception is either true or false. A holistic hermeneutics accepts and validates the realities of every life moment just as they are. In the dreams of individuals who are particularly prone to a dichotomous quality of consciousness and who lack psychic awareness of the here and now, blue light symbols can appear and point to an existential opening to a more unitary reality. In my own practice two clients have indeed presented blue light symbols. The two individuals have in common a Calvinistic Presbyterian background. Both of them had felt pressured by the idealistic value system, the essential effect of which was to disqualify the *de facto* reality of their lives.

The first client—a man in his early thirties from a rural family background—was a university psychologist. At the time, he was involved with the development of a catalogue of psychopathologies rated according to scientifically defined criteria of normality. In the course of the work he dreamt of "a mysterious figure wearing a luminescent blue crown." In the years following, he came to understand that his rural ancestry and Calvinistic inheritance had led him to overvalue the dualistic scientific approach that draws rigid lines between mental illness and health. He gradually opened to more expansive, a less judgmental approach to psychic life. We might consider the timeliness of this man's "luminescent blue crown" related to the current collective trend, whereby aspects of psychic life are increasingly banned to the realms of psychopathology. The symbol could indicate that the time has come for academia itself to go let of its "kingly" stance—its rationalistic, technocratic, ego-inflated approach—in favor of a more holistic view that ultimately sees humanity's "kingship" lying precisely in its respect toward the psyche and the rest of creation, as they are.

Even more striking is the childhood vision of a blue light, recalled by a woman in her fifties:

> I'd been to the little white village church where my younger sister had her confirmation. In the past I was confirmed by the same minister. Already at my own confirmation I had found the whole situation to be utter hypocrisy—the readings and preparation, and finally the church confirmation. But what I

now witnessed—squeezed between fat aunts in flowery dresses
and with the false singing choir in the background—was really
the bloody limit. I couldn't get away. After everyone had waved
goodbye and climbed into their cars and waved again, I arrived
with my parents at our family home. White table cloth, hand
plucked flowers from the garden, wide open veranda doors, guests
arriving, I went upstairs to my room utterly exhausted and
desperate about the fact that lies were winning over truth and
that there was nothing I could do about it, not even escape it. I
closed the door behind me and lay down on my bed—flat on
my stomach, arms stretched alongside my body. I don't recall,
but I think I cried, which in my view, back then, was quite
shameful. At a certain moment I felt that someone was standing
behind me. Feeling a bit startled I hastily lifted my head and
turned to look down to the left. Behind me, hanging in the air,
about one-and-a-half meters above the floor and thus a bit higher
up than me and not too close was a *blue light*. It was spinning
and created a circle of about twenty centimeters in diameter.
The intensity of the light and the high-speed spinning had such
a grabbing effect that I felt paralyzed or hypnotized—in any
case, nothing I'd ever experienced before. Then suddenly it faded
away and was gone. I kept looking at the spot where it had been
as if to plead it to come back, but it didn't. However it left me
with a felt sense, conviction really, that the reality of the spirit is
indestructible, that no religion or senseless rituals can take the
essence away. God is a living reality even in the worst places.

It would be possible here to diagnose a brief stress-induced psychotic
hallucination, a not atypical event of pre-puberty and, as it has not
recurred, leave it with that. But then we would fail to acknowledge
the meaning and relevance. The blue light seen by the child was, as
with the psychologist, a symbolic reaction to the collective, dualistic
Presbyterian and family value system. The religious dogmatism
determined if, when, and how god spoke to her, and it defined truth
and falsehood, the good and sinful. By contrast, the vision of the blue
light validated the young girl's instinctual revolt and affirmed her own
truth: objectively she was not bad or shameful. The spontaneous
appearance of the symbol not only compensated the dualistic
hermeneutics of her family complex. It also foretold also an opening
of consciousness, for destiny later led her to become a counselor to
the highest authorities of her country.

Here as in the fairy tale the blue light symbolizes the archetypal potential of continuous revelation, of a consciousness that is fully aware of the here and now and its unfathomable peaks and abysses. What about major revelations such as those manifested through Abraham, Moses, Jesus, Mohammed, and others? Like stones thrown into the water, they create waves that roll on for centuries, over and through history and over each other. My silence as a scientific observer is required before the "One whose Name cannot be uttered" (Yaweh); before "Allah," an appellation that abolishes itself in the Islamic creed, the *Shahada*: "la lha illa lha" ("there is not god but God"). But it might be that the origin of these revelations is also the unknowable origin of the "blue light," an image of the ever-enduring archetypal drive to live fully every here and now. As the Sufi mystic and philosopher 'Ibn Arabi wrote,

> God bestowed on us—through this state-of-arising . . . in which God constituted us in this path—the Face of the Truly Real . . . in everything. So for us, in our vision, there is nothing existing in the world but that we directly witness it with the Eye of the Truly Real . . . . So we do not blame anything at all in the world of being![7]

* * * *

To sum up: The notion of the "silence of god" typically constellates high expectations or misnomers concerning the meaning of life, with the source imagined to emanate from some metaphysical realm or from a mysterious "Self" deep within. This projection can easily overshadow our consciousness and acceptance of reality as it is. The blue light in the Grimm's fairy tale could be an archetypal image of the objective necessity to experience every here and now. The tale illustrates that the image is always present, underlying old habits as well as fresh perspectives, destructive impulses as well as the creative, the known as well as the unanticipated. *Not a single* episode in the tale, not one psychic constellation lacks the blue light's presence and availability. In other words, every single psychic condition *objectively* has its reason for being. The archetypal image of the blue light could point to the *fact* that all moments in life, including moments of unconsciousness, ARE consciousness transforming.

To accept the existential here and now is not to reject the value of clinical psychology and its causal, reductive, strategic, and efficiency oriented methods. We might however agree: clinical psychology's reliance on dichotomous, splitting categories like past/present, normal/abnormal, traumatizing/healing does nothing to serve the living psyche and the objective necessity for individuation. We have no other choice than to live life's every here and now—and this real existence constitutes what Jung calls "individuation."

We can conclude our reflections by looking again, but now from another perspective, at the title of my talk, "The Silence of 'God:'" There could be an absolute, usually silent mystery, which we as psychologists cannot speak about, which lies behind the ever present "blue light" archetype, and which endlessly induces the ego to live the reality/ies of life. To summon this mystery—which we can only grasp, doubt, or reject in the intimacy of faith—I offer some lines from a poem by an acquaintance of mine, the Swiss poet Jean-Marc Denervaud:[8]

Il n'y a que la mer	There is only the sea
Au-delà du jardin	Beyond the garden
Il n'y a que le silence	There is only the silence
Au-delà du silence	Beyond the silence

Al hamdul'Illah

NOTES

[1] See for instance, Wolfgang Giegerich, *The Flight into the Unconscious: An Analysis of C.G. Jung's Psychology Project, Collected English Papers Vol. 5* (New Orleans: Spring Journal Books, 2013).

[2] "The Blue Light," No. 116, *The Complete Grimm's Fairy Tales* (London: Routledge & Kegan Paul, 1975), pp. 530-534. In German see, "Das Blaue Licht," Nr. 116, *Kinder- und Hausmärchen*, gesammelt durch die Brüder Grimm (Munich: Artemis und Winkler, 1993), pp. 560-564.

[3] *Ibid.*, "The Blue Light," my summary. Author's note: In the standard English translation, the character helping the soldier is called "a black dwarf." Throughout, I replace it with "a little black man," the accurate translation of the original German, "*ein kleines schwarzes Männchen.*"

[4] Jean-Paul Sartre, *Nausea*, trans. Lloyd Alexander, Richard Howard (New York: New Directions, 2007). In French see, *La Nausée* [1938] (Paris: Gallimard, 1965).

[5] *Ibid.*, in *Nausea*, pp. 53-54; in *La Nausée*, p. 80.

[6] *Ibid.*, in *Nausea*, p. 131; in *La Nausée*, pp. 181-182; original emphases.

[7] 'Ibn Arabi, in James Winston Morris, "'Seeking God's Face:' 'Ibn Arabi on Right Action and Theophanic Vision: Part 2," in *Journal of the Muhyiddin 'Ibn Arabi Society*, Vol. 17, Oxford 1995, p. 2.

[8] Jean-Marc Denervaud, "Il n'y a que la mer...," in *Au delà du portail* (Geneva: Arttesia Diffusion, Samizdat Publishing, 2012), p. 10, the original French with my translation reprinted by the kind permission of Editions Samizdat.

4

Silence is Unbearable
Make More Noise!

Allan Guggenbühl

T he injunction to "make more noise" surely sounds absurd. Don't we dread, even hate, noise? Our sleep is disturbed when neighbors celebrate the victory of their local soccer team with boisterous song, loud music, and shouting. The rumble of aircraft flying overhead distracts our conversation with colleagues or a psychotherapy session. The din in the pub drowns out our friends' words. We all seem to agree: noise is something we want to avoid. Moments of silence are cherished as a chance to reflect, to mull things over, to do some deep thinking. To now contemplate the value of noise is not to depreciate silence. But while we treasure silence, we ought to consider that psychologically noise is just as important. In this essay I go so far as to argue that exposure to a certain amount of noise guarantees our emotional wellbeing and social stability.

Not so long ago my conflict management institute was asked to help decrease conflict on Swiss trains. As we had been told, the staff was repeatedly confronted with violent, often drunken passengers. Several incidents involved passengers who were caught without tickets, and then spat in the faces of the ticket controllers, bit their hands, or attacked them verbally. Our job was to train the personnel to prevent escalations by dealing more consciously with these situations. Studying reports and holding interviews, we aimed first to determine where the conflicts were most likely to occur. As we discovered, it was not in the second class carriages (likely to be crowded with families and groups of adolescents), nor in the first class (often occupied by people conducting business while underway). Rather, we were astonished to find the highest incidence of conflict occurring in the silent carriages—the quiet zones, innovatively designated as such by the Swiss Federal Railway!

How could this be, we wondered, when the passengers who travel in these quiet cars freely consent to refrain from disturbing others, agreeing not to talk or use cell phones and other noisy devices? As it emerged, instead of providing the desired silence and tranquility, these quiet zones transformed many passengers into uneasy curmudgeons, ready to clash noisily with their fellow travelers at the drop of a hat. They felt entitled to combat whenever they heard a sound—even if it were nothing more than the shuffling of papers, a loud sneeze, or a sighing yawn. Reluctantly the Swiss Federal Railway decided to abandon the quiet zones, at least in the second class carriages.

It is worth considering that, at a most basic level, our very perception of noise connects us with our surroundings, even with natural events that may be otherwise imperceptible: Hearing itself depends on invisible airwaves that enter our ear tunnel and become translated into brain impulses through highly complex processes. These airwaves are created by physical events that transpire around us. For instance whether we realize it or not, the rumble of thunder links us to an atmospheric explosion of air caused by lightning. The chirping of crickets connects us with stridulation, the rubbing of wing on wing. In the audible sigh of a colleague we apprehend the sound of air rushing invisibly out of his lungs. With the sound of a splash, we register that an object has fallen into liquid. In other words, just as sound waves registered as noise connect us with surrounding events, the sound profile itself mirrors the nature of those events, helping to orient us to our surroundings. Sound helps to identify what is around us.

Mother Earth herself produces sound waves through physical processes that we perceive as noise, as when water freezes, expands, and causes the audible crack of stones breaking up. Or when ascending air releases rain that resounds on the earth's surface as the patter of a summer shower. But above the hubbub of our everyday lives, the natural sounds of our blue planet often go unnoticed, or are hardly discernable. Under ordinary weather conditions at the top of a peak in the Alps, one strains to hear much of anything. The silence is broken only intermittently by the noise of rocks tumbling down into a valley, or maybe a whistling wind. Of course a good deal of noise would confront us, should we stand on the rim of an active volcano, or cling to the ground in the midst of a tornado, or dash for shelter during a thunderstorm. When such conditions are absent, our natural surroundings can be incredibly quiet, sometimes unbearably so.

I have in mind a place in Antarctica that has been likened to Mars, the McMurdo Dry Valleys. One of our planet's most arid and extreme cold deserts, the region is nearly devoid of life except for the simplest plants and microorganisms. Accordingly, the McMurdo Dry Valleys are extremely quiet—so quiet, some say, that the silence is heard "as audible stillness,"[1] and "you can hear the machinations of your own body."[2] Two geologists of the Polytechnic Institute of the University of Zürich (ETH) had the opportunity to undertake field research in this place.[3] What they hadn't realized was that the silence would become unbearable—so much so, that after a time it caused them to become often angry at one another and soon their relationship deteriorated into mutual detest. It seems that the intense silence had the effect of enlarging the slightest and most banal sounds, such that the smallest noise made by one became for the other an extreme irritation and cause to quarrel: the rhythmic slapping of a loose strap on a rucksack; heavy breathing; a scratching of the nose.

As the silence was unbearable to the two experienced fieldworkers—not to mention the curmudgeons in the silent zones of the Swiss trains—it might well be asked, could we have endured the original quietness of our planet? Or, how much quietude are we designed to withstand? Living beings of all kinds interrupted the earth's ur-silence, making the planet a much noisier place. Bees humming, lions roaring, and dogs barking send signals that mark territory, attract mates, and distinguish friend from foe. The variety of animal noises is remarkable. The Australian jungle Lyrebird for instance has its own uniquely beautiful call but also specializes in imitating nearly any sound it hears. So when the bird strays into an urban area, it picks up the sounds—to perfectly replicate them at home, flabbergasting hikers who would never expect to hear machine drills, honking horns, or police car sirens emanating from the jungle!

If silence is on one hand desired and difficult to obtain, why should it be the cause of such distress? Could it be that our yearning and demands for silence cause us to deny the archetypal value of noise? Let us consider that our majority enters this world not quietly, but with a scream that gains the welcoming attention of everyone around. We soon begin to signal other signs of life—a fart, a grunt, a gurgle, a laugh. Eventually we learn to sing, whistle, produce sound on musical instruments, and of course we gradually acquire language, progressing ever more into the realm of culturally coded noise.

The internalized sounds of our group, clan, nation, or region contribute to our sense of identity, and who is friend, who is foe. And uttered speech allows us to apprehend distinctions embedded within any given language, dialect, or regional accent. We Swiss German speakers recognize a native of the Canton of Bern when we hear "Modi," for "girl"—while "Mädchen" tips us off that a Zürcher is in our midst. When we hear "Botsche" instead of "Buebe" for "boy," we register the presence of a compatriot from the Valais. Sub-groups distinguish themselves with further sound profiles contained in jargon, colloquialisms, and the like. People speaking computerese may be identified by outsiders as nerds; those who use legalese are detectable as lawyers; psychologists are often said to reveal themselves with psychobabble. Our talk can disclose whether we are bankers, social workers, or if we belong to an older generation. It allows us to express and transmit ideas, images, and psychological projections. It enables us to go beyond our subjective here-and-now, to share this world and its realities with others.

Indeed according to the anthropologist and evolutionary psychologist Robin Dunbar, human noise making has evolved for a purpose far more natural than that of transmitting pragmatic messages and sophisticated communications.[4] His conclusion takes into account the chimpanzees, among other primates, who ordinarily spend a good deal of time grooming each other and engaging in rough and tumble play, all accompanied by grunting, chattering, squealing. The superficial judgment we could render is that the chimps are wasting their time. Apparently this interpretation is wrong: It was discovered that when chimpanzees are deprived of leisure—time to simply fool around with each other—the frequency of their bullying increases. Bullying among chimpanzees can be brutal indeed and provoked for no apparent reason. It seems to take little more than a chimp's awkward movement or other odd behavior to elicit a gang attack, when co-members of the troop grab him by the arms and legs and tear him apart, causing a gruesome death. Conversely, the bullying decreases when chimps have adequate time for grooming and play—"quality time" in today's parlance—for this seemingly meaningless activity serves the purpose of forging mutual bonds and sustaining group cohesion.

Furthermore Dunbar introduces recent research suggesting that the Neanderthal peoples themselves were not overwhelmingly pressured to find shelter and food. So they were more sedentary, with more leisure time on their hands, than has been supposed. Most surprising, the research shows that the Neanderthals had the physical apparatus for speech, which they seem to have used, however primitively. Thus they, too, developed social bonds as they devoted good parts of the day to mutual back scratching, playful chasing—and now joking around. Moving on in the course of evolution, humans gradually subsumed grooming and play to language, substituting much of the physical contact not only with speech as such. As Dunbar sees it, it is the noise we make as idle talk or gossip that contributes substantially to the fulfillment of our essential needs for emotional bonding and social cohesion.[5] "If being human is all about talking," Dunbar observes,

> it's the tittle tattle of life that makes the world go round, not the pearls of wisdom that fall from the lips of the Aristotles and the Einsteins. We are social beings—and our world—no less than that of the monkeys and apes—is cocooned in the interests and minutiae of everyday life. They fascinate us beyond measure.[6]

Our move from the savannahs and forests to well-constructed habitats means that we no longer need sleep under the stars or suffer exposure to the cold or torrential rains. The comforts of civilization, however, come at the price of increased noise. The racket of tools, cars, aircraft, washing machines, sirens, alarms, and slamming doors are daily fare in contemporary life. Contrary to popular belief, though, modernization has not made of our society the noisiest.

To grasp this reality we can imaginatively transport ourselves into the fifteenth century. Landing, say, in the medieval Swiss countryside, we find lone-standing farmhouses and fewer forests and roads than we would today. Moving on, we come upon walled-in towns, barricaded from human foes and nature. The buildings stand close together, communal space is narrow, and the streets are crowded and squalid. Now, we might have imagined these medieval towns to be idyllically quiet, bucolic places, with people strolling leisurely on the streets, tending to their daily errands. To the contrary, we find ourselves in the midst of immense stench and noise. We hear the penetrating voice of the town crier, and people in the market shouting and screaming as they compete to sell their wares. The clattering of hooves and the clanging of wheels on cobble stone create such a din that we can hardly hear our own voices. It is a turbulent and rowdy place. Thanks to these noises the residents were constantly reminded of the efforts needed to create a safe habitat. Day by day the people registered the enormous energy that was required to keep their civilization intact.

When trains started rolling on tracks throughout Europe their unusual noises fascinated children and adults alike: the hissing engines, the clattering wheels, the blowing whistles, the screeching breaks. These evocative sounds contributed to the rise of the train as a symbol of our conquest of nature. Extremely noisy aircraft, like the Lockheed Super Constellation or the Boeing 707 making their maiden flights from the Zürich airport, captivated audiences of thousands. The roaring sports car has long been a symbol of masculine power. But today's collective generally wants vehicles that run smoothly and silently. We no longer wish to be reminded that machines produce energy for us. The tools we construct to exploit our blue planet should now remain discreetly, delusionally, in the background.

Nevertheless some urban noises persist or seem to be produced deliberately, as if to assert a message. In Switzerland the construction workers assigned to tear up the streets typically activate their extremely noisy drills at 7:00 am in the morning. If someone has the impudence to still be asleep at that hour, he or she is reminded rather brutally that other people are already up and working! Apparently this demonstrative act serves to hamper social unrest, for it demands our acknowledgement of the workmen who are at labor in the public interest. Most often they stop their machines at 7:15 am, having gained the desired attention . . .

Young people often deploy a similar strategy, asserting their presence with sound emissions that aggravate society's more aged members. In the 1930's it was jazz, considered by the older generation to be vile and cause for fear that this "Negro" music would lead to degeneration of the brain.[7] In the 1950's the debauched and dangerous noise came from rock n' roll, which was followed by other irritants like pop, hip hop, reggae, house music. A year ago a young adolescent, with whom I had a good therapeutic connection, wanted to introduce me to a rapper he admired. He handed me one of his earphones so we could listen together. When I remarked that the rap sounded rather conventional, the young man directed me to listen to the lyrics. Stunned by the blunt words, full of racism and sexism, I handed back the earphone, noting in a stern tone my disagreement with the malicious text. He gazed at me, looking very puzzled, as if thinking, "This guy doesn't get it!" At that moment a gap opened between us and I suddenly felt old. I, feeling convinced in my judgment, found myself participating with him in an old ritual by which sound serves to identify, demarcate, and put distance between the generations.

The ritual of psychotherapy per se generates an acoustic sphere, the specific nature or quality of which unfolds by a mutual interplay of sounds. As such, a psychotherapy session has much in common with music, which is noise cultivated for its own sake. Creating and listening to music connects us with our inner realms as well as with others, evoking feelings, fantasies, and sensations, and influencing our moods. Likewise, in the spirit of a jam session or Dunbar's "idle talk," the verbal exchange between psychotherapist and patient serves more than the purpose of goal-oriented, rational communication. As we understand, however, the sounds created during a psychotherapy session are not intended for an outer world, but specifically and exclusively for the attending players.

* * * *

The sounds of nature, of humans, urban noises, and of course music are part of our collective psyche and resonate in our souls. Indeed, as myth axiomatically reflects our behavior patterns and complexes, it symbolizes our archetypal rootedness in noise. Take for example Pan— the truly raucous, mischievous, and sometimes terrifying god. He roams the woods and fields on his goat haunches, startling everyone in his path with the sound of his emblematic flute. Pan personifies our instinctual urge to produce noise, while his effect on others evidences our self-protective reaction to overwhelming sound—but he can just as much lead us to our inner, playful child. Dionysus—god of wine and ritual madness—lures us to let go, to join the group in boisterous song and dance, to share with others a shedding of everyday duties and sorrows. Finally we might think of Apollo—the ever youthful and rational sun god and patron of poetry and music. He perhaps especially bespeaks the ability to transform noise into music, to make sense of raw and often inchoate sounds.

Such archetypal figures, each in their own way, urge us to refrain from banning noise, challenging us instead to attune to the sounds around us as music and to have some fun with it as we go along. This we might try to do the next time we register incoherent utterances from our patients, or when an airplane roars by—or when we overhear a yawn, quarrel, or story as we sit in a train, bus, or pub or when we wander through a market place, a shopping center, or public garden. "What song is this?" we might ask; "in what jam, in what concert, in what symphony do I take part?" Psychologically this kind of encounter embeds us in the collective to which we belong.

There is no denying the value of silence. As a contrast to everyday life it offers respite, helps us to reflect and to get in touch with ourselves. The ritual practice of silence is of course one among the known pathways to spiritual enlightenment. But for the average mortal, long-enduring or complete quietude is unbearable. Too much silence isolates us, breaks us down. The noises emanated by our fellow humans and civilization connect us with one another; they regulate our thinking and serve as normalizers, compensating existential fears and helping to keep us from going crazy. Finally, the noises we hear and emit ground us as actors in the dramas rehearsed on this earth by a larger invisible author, the *anima mundi*, allowing us to cherish the illusion of having some kind of permanency on this lonely planet. In the long term, the feeling of oneness that we long for arises from our immersion in the noise that we make.

NOTES

[1] Alia Kahn, "How One Scientist Caught Polar Fever" (April 11, 1013), in *Women's Adventure Magazine* at Antiarcticahttp://www.womensadventuremagazine.com/extreme-outdoors/its-personal-holidays-in-antarctica/ (accessed November 19, 2013).

[2] Chris Kannen, "Whatever Moves or Makes Noise," in *ARID: A Journal of Design, Art, and Ecology* at http://aridjournal.com/whatever-moves-or-makes-noise-chris-kannen/ (accessed November 19, 2013).

[3] Personal information provided by Dr. G. Wyssling, Geologist & Explorer (Pfaffhausen, Switzerland).

[4] Robin Dunbar, *Grooming, Gossip and the Evolution of Language* (Cambridge, MA: Harvard University Press, 1996).

[5] *Ibid.*, pp. 164-168.

[6] *Ibid.*, p. 4.

[7] See for example, Michael H. Kater, *Different Drummers, Jazz in the Culture of Nazi Germany* (Oxford: Oxford University Press, 2003). See also, Richard J. Lawn, *Experiencing Jazz*, 2nd Ed. (New York: Routledge, 2013), pp. 78-79. In German see, Bernd Polster, *Swing Heil—Jazz im Nationalsozialismus* (Berlin: Transit, 1989). See also Ekkehard Jost, *Sozialgeschichte des Jazz in den USA* (Frankfurt am Main: Fischer, 1982).

5

The Legend of the Wandering Jew
Pilgrimage and Embodied Spirituality

Waltraud Körner

INTRODUCTION[1]

W e live in a time when people are fond of wandering, at least in Europe, where many are especially attracted to the old pilgrims' routes. Among the most famous is the "Way of St. James," which actually consists of many paths with points of origin all over Europe.[2] One of them passes straight through Kartause Ittingen, the place of this year's Jungian Odyssey. Typically travelling hundreds or even thousands of kilometers and being underway for weeks or months at a time, modern day pilgrims finally reach the place where all paths converge into one, which leads to Santiago de Compostela, the renowned cathedral in northwestern Spain. According to Christian legend, the city of Santiago was the final station in James's pilgrimage, and the cathedral the place of his burial. The Way of St. James, known also as the "Milky Way," has inspired the creation of novels, stories, and movies, suggesting the broad collective interest in pilgrimage as such.

Among my favorites is the lovely French film entitled, *Saint Jacques ... La Meque*, distributed in English as *Start Walking*.[3] This is the realistic but fictional story of a pilgrimage undertaken by the bitterly estranged sons and daughters of an old mother who pretends to be dead. Her last will and testament obliges the siblings and their partners to walk together to Santiago with a professional guide. Initially they are motivated by nothing but greed, for only if they go and arrive together at the cathedral will they collect their huge inheritance. Along the way they are joined by others, for instance a Mid-Eastern boy who believes they are on the way to Mecca. As one can imagine, the journey is not easy, but each of the sojourners undergoes inner development with both painful and funny experiences. It is a story that made me cry and laugh at the same time!

Long being an avid pilgrim myself, my research on the topic began many years ago at an Eranos conference, where the participants shared their experiences of a new English translation of the *I Ching*. At this event the hexagram that repeatedly occurred to me was number fifty-six, "Sojourning," or in other translations, "The Wanderer." "To be in accord with the time," it says, "you are told to: *sojourn!*" [4] Although I myself have not yet made it to the cathedral in Santiago de Compostela, I did journey to Andalusia with a small group of women under the guidance of a modern mystic who is also a spiritual healer. Each morning we set out to walk the same mountain pathway. Along this rather short path—about one kilometer—we stopped at several stations, attuning to what might arise from the unconscious, both our own and that of our guide. Every day the guide walked with each of us, one after the other, initiating processes that would increase our self-knowledge and devotion to our souls and destinies. Our journey was indeed a pilgrimage and learning process, sometimes very painful, sometimes consoling. In the evenings, when we women gathered without our guide, we realized that many complexes were constellated, and relied on one another to ground ourselves.

Among the impressions that have remained with me is that of the value of wandering as a kind of meditation. The length of the route, however, is unimportant. The main thing is the inner experience and meaning—in Jungian terms, an encounter with the Self. A precondition for this journey, says the hexagram, is to "understand and accept" the body as our ultimate place of "dwelling." With this in mind, I would suggest that, consciously or unconsciously, it is a longing to be in touch with an *embodied* Self that compels many if not most of today's wanderers and pilgrims. Now, the hexagram points as well to a ritual preparedness and spiritual unfolding, which amount to feelings and events that are familiar to us as elements of an individuation process:

Wandering entails "sacrifice"—a "letting-go" of home, of "willful intention," and all "certainties." We then experience ourselves as "exiles" undergoing "punishment . . . for severe offenses." Rather than resisting, we "grow" by accepting the situation as a "test by ordeal." As the hexagram advises, "mingling with others as a stranger whose identity comes from a distant center is the adequate way to handle it." To survive, we learn to "flexibly adapt to what crosses our path," to "move in harmony with the vicissitudes of life" and with "continually changing awareness." We become "quiet and attentive," turning inwardly to our "hearts," our "truth." All of this, while wandering—and while simultaneously "articulating inner limits," for these limits "provide the stable base" from which we can "face inner and outer changes."

To my mind, the *I Ching's* archetypal wanderer echoes our nomadic origins, and especially the exodus and diasporic life of the Jewish people. Thus I have come to see in the figure of the eternally Wandering Jew a personification of the archetype that offers particular meaning for our day and age. The Legend of the Wandering Jew, which we shall soon explore, is a Christian tale of late Antiquity. While the literary origins are uncertain, the central motif, eternal wandering, is speculated to have roots in Teutonic legend and the New Testament, for instance. Parallels are drawn as well with the biblical Cain, who was banished for the crime of fratricide to roam in the land of Nod. I say this, acknowledging the appropriation of Jewish history and scripture by the early Christian Church—and most grievously, by the forces of anti-Semitism. I will go only briefly into these dimensions, however, as they have been researched in depth by many scholars.[5]

Most importantly in my view, behind the Wandering Jew of Christian legend is the wandering God who has been with us since Yaweh left the temple to accompany the Jewish exodus and diaspora. Thus we should not be surprised to find that a "precursor" to the legend's protagonist has been recognized in Elijah, he being by "Talmudic tradition . . . . the eternal Jew who would lead the people of Israel back to their land."[6] Writing in 1921, well before the rise of the Third Reich, C.G. Jung remarked, "the Legend of the Wandering Jew,"

> [p]sychologically, sprang from a component of the personality, or a charge of libido that could find no outlet in the Christian attitude to life and the world and was therefore repressed. The Jews were always a symbol for this, hence the persecution mania against the Jews in the Middle Ages. . . .[7]

In other words: The legend projects a Christian shadow that maligns certain qualities of the Jewish "personality." Given that the original Christians themselves were Jews, we can well suppose that the rise of the Christian Church brought a collective disidentification with these qualities. And so they were gradually split off and projected upon the Jews—initially to explain their "difference," and later to justify their persecution. Divesting the Wandering Jew of this shadow and the Christian context, I find him very apt to symbolize a wanderer's mode of spirituality, one that can be as meaningful for people who feel compelled or choose to wander as it may be for today's exiles and migrants.

THE LEGEND: AN EXPLORATION

Over the course of centuries, stories spread by word-of-mouth, purporting meetings with a man from Jerusalem who was strikingly tall, and wondrous in many ways. He had witnessed Christ's crucifixion, it was said, and ever since he had been spotted walking throughout Europe, the Mid-East, and eventually North America. The oldest extant chronicles, based on oral tradition and scattered letters, come to us from thirteenth century Catholic monks whose writings in Latin record encounters that date to around 1228.[8] An alleged meeting in the winter of 1542 with the Bishop of Schleswig, Paulus von Eitzen, is the subject of the pamphlet, *Short Description and Story of a Jew By the Name of Ahasverus* (*Kurtze beschreibung und Erzehlung / von einem Juden / mit Namen Ahasverus*).[9] At first published anonymously in 1602 by a German Protestant theologian, this was the first chronicle to identify the wanderer as a Jew, and the first to call him "Ahasverus," or often translated, "Ahasver."[10] It moreover attested that the man was a shoemaker by trade, and about fifty years old when he spoke with the bishop. The above and all later variants differ in other details as well, but they all agree, in a nutshell, as follows:

> When Christ was on the way to the crucifixion and stopped to rest, the man was overcome with righteous zeal and cried, "Pack off! Get on to where you are supposed to be!" Christ sternly augured, "I will stand and rest, but you shall walk [the earth until Judgment Day]." On that same day the man left his family behind, hastening with the crowd to Calvary to see the execution of this heretic and seducer. To his surprise, after witnessing the cruel spectacle he was unable to re-enter Jerusalem. Since then he has been walking in foreign lands, one after another.
>
> Wherever the man is seen, he is always barefooted, and his grey hair hangs down over his shoulders. He always wears the same trousers, the same knee-length frock, and a coat that reaches to his feet. In church he listens with such devotion to the sermons that he seems to not move at all, unless it be to bow and smite his breast when Christ's name is spoken.
>
> Wherever he sojourns, he always mingles with the people, and instantly speaks their language as if it were his own. Being abstemious, he contents himself with little food and drink. The few coins he accepts, he gives to the poor, trusting that God will provide for him. He is never seen laughing. Indeed he is quiet, except when answering questions or when pained by those who curse or blaspheme God with mockery of Christ's suffering. Reading copiously and listening fervently, he exceeds all ecclesiasts and historians with his vast knowledge of world history, religions, governments and current events, and he was able to predict the future. Each time he reaches the age of one hundred, he faints, and awakens at the age he had been at the time of the crucifixion.
>
> He knows not what God has in store for him, unless at the Last Judgment he should be a living witness to Christ's passion, to convince more of the unbelieving and the godless. And he wants to suffer his own portion until God calls him to peace from this vale of tears. . . .[11]

The 1602 chronicle would become the most frequently re-embellished, translated, and re-published, and thus also the most widely disseminated, well into the next century. Briefly said, among its effects was to re-instill in the popular imagination a link between the Wandering Jew and Judas Iscariot. It thereby supported the spread of longstanding anti-Judaic beliefs that the Jews betrayed Christ, and the Jewish destiny of homelessness would prevail as punishment for the unrepentant. With this, the story also contributed to the spreading of negative Jewish stereotypes that would lay the ground for virulent anti-Semitism and set the stage for the Sho'ah. Along the way, the Nazis themselves appropriated the legend, making pernicious slurs of the term "eternal Jew" and the name "Ahasver;" this codified *Judenhass* was then extended to mean also gypsies, homosexuals, the mentally ill, avant-garde artists, and all others deemed to be "'not just benignly different, but malevolent and corrosive.'"[12]

However, prior to the advent of German National Socialism, a change had taken place, perhaps a germinal evolution of collective consciousness: The Napoleonic and Industrial revolutions, and finally Romanticism, caused the legend in some sectors to be "separated from its . . . Christian context," allowing positive and negative associations to go side by side.[13] In the positive sense, the Wandering Jew held the status of what could be called the archetypal lowly hero, for he symbolized values that were emerging and embodied only at the fringes of the dominant collective. For instance: the passion for wandering as such, antiauthoritarianism, lasting freedom and mobility, individualism, liberal intellect, creative suffering, entrepreneurship—but here I am jumping ahead.

For the time being, I want to emphasize that across cultures and eras, in myth and legend, the motif of eternal movement holds ambivalent meaning. It does indeed often appear as punishment for blasphemy against a deity, or for pride and presumption against a god or against nature. We have already mentioned the biblical Cain. Sisyphus, as we know, was condemned to forever roll a huge boulder up a hill. Ixion, king of the Greek Lapiths, was banned for eternity, his body bound to an endlessly spinning, fiery wheel. Tantalus, a son of Zeus, was forced to stand forever in the abyss of Tartarus, perpetually grasping for unobtainable water and food. A seventeenth century nautical legend is about the Flying Dutchman, the ship whose captain was doomed to endless sailing.[14] An early nineteenth century American legend tells of Peter Rugg, the Missing Man, who was damned to ride forever, his carriage driving always in the opposite direction than Rugg wanted to go.[15]

Psychologically, the punishing movement in such stories suggests a paradoxical, humiliating condition of stasis in that it leads to no hope, no change, no development or redemption. It could picture a state of possession by the unconscious resulting from the betrayal of the Self in favor of self-righteousness or inflated ego consciousness. We could speak as well of failed *metanoia*. That is, the failure of a self-healing process, whereby the dissolution of the ego could point toward a renewal of consciousness by an autonomous, inward-turning of the psyche toward the Divine or the Self, the regulator of both collective and individual development. In this light, how might we interpret the fate of the eternally Wandering Jew? Does his indestructible body represent an inescapable curse, or failed *metanoia*, or rather a kind of blessing?

Like a folk tale figure identified initially with the reigning old king, "the man of Jerusalem" at first identifies with the ruling powers of the land. Thus his anger and vengefulness mirror the collective rejection of the "Other," here represented by Christ, himself a Jew, condemned to death for his heretical claim to being the Messiah and Son of God. For his own contempt the man appears to have been doomed to wander until Judgment Day. However, in the course, we discern changes of the kind that resemble an individuation journey, which transpires rather typically by painful sacrifice, beginning with a humbling of the ego:

To the man's surprise, his witnessing of Christ's cruel death brings a change of heart, his sorrow and compassion for the Other flows forth. In the "just so" spirit of folk tale, we would say that wandering as such constellates further transformation. For it is implicitly this movement, step by step, year by year, that makes of the once punished man a hermitic wanderer or pilgrim, who grows ever more inward, humble, pious, charitable, and well read. In touch with the earth, exposed to the elements, forbearing, yet longing for peace, he seems not so much to be stuck, possessed, or destitute, but to acquire the traits of the *I Ching's* sojourner: the itinerant stranger, led by his heart and inner truth, tested by ordeal, mingling with others, moving in harmony with the vicissitudes of life. Moreover, with the passing of centuries, the Wandering Jew manifests miraculous attributes: omnipresence, spontaneous multi-linguality, all-knowingness, and eternality. Such features by all means suggest this eternal wanderer's place among archetypal figures like Elijah, and also Moses, Christ, the Islamic saint Al-Qadir, and the Mesopotamian King Gilgamesh—wanderers who evolve mana-personalities, numinously irradiating the wisdom and wholeness of the Divine, or the Jungian Self.

My reading as such, while coming from a Jungian perspective, is not entirely new. In 1902, the Austrian Jewish thinker Nathan Birnbaum, finding himself cut off from Zionism, published a poem cycle that,

> express[es] the tension embodied in the figure of the Ahasver—the tension between vitality and decline and death, between hope and love and pessimism and vengefulness.... [Here] [t]he Wandering Jew turns into a spiritual, Jesus-like figure that redeems the world by his exile as he bestows the gift of love on his haters and opponents.[16]

As the Wandering Jew appears in contemporary pictures, stories, poems, and novels—far too many to name here—he often again stands inspirationally for the immortal wanderer who can appear at any time and place.[17] The twentieth century German author Marie Luise Kaschnitz (1901-1974) captures the image when she poetically envisions her own sighting of Ahasver in London at the Hotel Ritz. Here, Kaschnitz sees him on the verge of suicide: "Why? He had had enough. / He was fifty years old or fifty thousand." Alone and lonely, he listened in vain for the voices of friends. He wore a "silk shirt," which hid the many "scars and weals" on his back—a "map of suffering." "[H]is knees were swollen," "one foot was lame," "his brow etched with escape routes." Having drunk his bitter suicidal tea, he sank blissfully into his deathbed. "Only he forgot, unfortunately, to shut the door." Awakening to rescue, encircled by his "beautiful chiding daughters," Mr. Ahasver says, 'I was sleeping so poorly.'"[18]

Such stories and life experiences remind us that those who are exiled—by war, genocide, religious, economic, or social conditions, natural disaster, or even by force of their own psyches—often bear the shadow of our collective value systems. Our effort to take back negative projections would be a small, not to say easy, step toward dissolving the perception of the migrant, the refugee, or any Other who seems to threaten our wellbeing. Likewise we could better offer hospitality to these itinerant guests—including our respect for their mythology, beliefs, and inner destinies. In other words, we could embrace the *I Ching's* wisdom: The wanderer's ability to let go rests on his or her "loyalty to a symbol," be it an idea, a hope, or a memory—some kind of center or stable base, which can be carried along. Deuteronomy depicts it in the form of a covenant between God and the Jewish people. Envisioning the promised home, the covenant attests to the legacy of exile and diaspora, to which belongs also the duty of a tithe, an offering and sacrifice that preserves the humble relationship of the wanderer to the Divine:

> (1) And it shall be, when thou art come in unto the land which the Lord thy God giveth thee *for* an inheritance, and possessest it, and dwellest therein; (2) That thou shalt take of the first of all the fruit of the earth, which thou shalt bring of thy land that the Lord thy God giveth thee, and shalt put *it* in a basket, and shalt go unto the place which the Lord thy God shall choose to place his name there. (3) And thou shalt go unto the priest . . . , and say unto him, I profess this day unto the Lord thy God, that I am come unto the country which the Lord sware unto our fathers for to give us. (4) And the priest shall take the basket . . . , and set it down before the altar of the Lord thy God. (5) And thou shalt . . . say before the Lord thy God, A Syrian ready to perish *was* my father, and he went down into Egypt, and sojourned there with a few, and became there a nation, great, mighty, and populous . . .[19]

For some people though, the prospect of "mingling with others as a stranger" is perhaps too optimistic. Sometimes the centering yet distant home may no longer exist, or return may be permanently denied. All the more so would the prolonged suffering of separation, adaptation, and negative projections stand to alienate one from an inwardly carried center.

Kaschnitz's Ahasver, being in certain ways oh-so-human, provides hope. Like the Wandering Jew of the legend in general, he appears to have an indestructible body. Recalling the *I Ching's* "ultimate place of dwelling," this body is the locus of divine intervention, the material place in which life transcends the desire for death, kinship transcends isolation, love and hope transcend despair. The poet would seem to illuminate on one hand the Jewish destiny of spiritual forbearance—and on the other hand, the Judaic belief in the body itself as a sustaining, sacred center. The image as such gives us pause to reconsider the power of the Wandering Jew to elicit positive projections, albeit sometimes idealizing ones. Or, to put it slightly differently: we discern in him the spiritual life of the wanderer, which—split off in the collective Christian attitude—may give rise to unconscious envy of the Jews. Accordingly it would spark unconscious longings, for instance, to escape a dominant ego; to shed material attachments; to roam freely; to be close to the earth; to discover growth in suffering; to obtain inner steadfastness. And most of all: to carry the flow of the spiritual and eternal *in this earthly and bodily life, wherever we might wander.* Here we would find a creative and loving source that would move us toward the experience of greater depth.

PERSONAL PILGRIMAGE

As we are all originally nomads and wanderers, often exiled even from ourselves, the Wandering Jew is an especially apt image that can inspire and guide our personal spiritual sojourns. Some of us may walk with others, to share a sense of community; others will go alone. Either way, I am persuaded the purpose is best served when the journey is physical. Bodily engagement helps to anchor the process and keep us in touch with the earth, our common original home. And as Jung observed, the Self is both physical and spiritual, and "[t]he symbols of the Self arise from the body..."[20] Along similar lines the Jungian dance therapist Joan Chodorow emphasizes,

> It is important to remember that the earliest experience we have of consciousness is through the body. Physical consciousness is the foundation from which we continue to develop psychologically.[21]

As we grow psychologically, so the Self also calls us to grow spiritually. And to move physically can be to experience the Self in a most primal way, to become almost naked in our expression of emotion and the stirrings of the spirit within.

Chodorow's work brings me to note that the physical journey need not necessarily take the form of hiking or walking. Just as we are all originally wanderers, so are we all originally dancers, for instance. We might dance intentionally to become filled with the divine spirit, like the dervishes of Konya who whirl themselves into trance. The sheikh, as the leader and witness of the ritual, gives a sign to end the whirling when he observes the energy diminishing, when the dancers might exceed their physical limits. To conceive it the other way around, the divine creative spirit moves our bodies, which seem to know best how to experience its truth. In this sense I am reminded of King David's spontaneous dance of joy, as relayed in the Book of Samuel:

> (16) [A]s the ark of the Lord came into the city of David, Michal Saul's daughter looked through a window, and saw king David leaping and dancing before the Lord; and she despised him in her heart. (17) And they brought in the ark of the Lord, and set it . . . in the midst of the tabernacle . . . : and David offered burnt offerings and peace offerings before the Lord. . . . (20) Then . . . . Michal . . . came out to meet David, and said, How glorious was the king of Israel to day, who uncovered himself . . . in the eyes of the handmaids of his servants, as one of the vain fellows shamelessly uncovereth himself! (21) And David said unto Michal, *It was* before the Lord, which chose me before thy father, and before all his house, to appoint me ruler over the people of the Lord, over Israel: therefore will I play before the Lord. (22) And I will yet be more vile than thus, and . . . base in mine own sight: and of the maidservants which thou hast spoken of, . . . shall I be had in honour.[22]

Taking the Wandering Jew as a symbol and guide, the spiritual sojourner endures loneliness and the unknown, and devotes endless attention to the slightest perceptions of meaning. From the standpoint of Jungian psychology, pilgrimage is always somehow a search for one's true sense of the Self and connectedness with the cosmos, the surrounding flow of life. Indeed our humanity is based on our readiness to experience the stream and the wholeness of life, starting with our first steps in childhood. Invisibly accompanying us on our way, the Self and its messages manifest themselves especially in times of distress, when we are most at a loss of meaning.

It follows that the pilgrim typically asks, "Who am I, really?" Of course "I" tread the soil with my own feet, but my self-awareness, my inner sense of being, changes as new thoughts and emotions arise. My horizon broadens if I can accept the transformation of my relationship to myself and to others. But let us recall the *I Ching's* instruction to "articulate inner limits." The text here asks for our honest assessment of personal resources, both the bodily and the psychological, to lessen the risk of exhaustion, or of losing the path to our true identities, desires, and emotions.

That said, in the western world, our clinging to stability and settledness seems to hinder our opening to the wanderer's way. We may fear being robbed of our identity, and we seem often unable to share our lives with strangers. Are we too greatly afraid to let go, to experience the unknown? It is my impression that the covenant in Deuteronomy attempts to balance the inclination to settle by summoning the memory of the exiled father, who established the legacy of the Jews as a nation of wanderers.

Conclusion

The Wandering Jew—humble, compassionate, and with no home but the road—seems to embody our forgotten human essence and identity as exiles and wanderers. We are perhaps not so different from the animals that migrate in search of food. Yet "The Wanderer" is by definition one who travels without a fixed course, aim, or goal. So like the Wandering Jew, who knew not where he was headed or what the future would hold on the day he departed from Calvary, as spiritual pilgrims we need remain open to the unknown. As we travel, the struggle for self-knowledge—the continuous looking into the shaft of our souls—keeps us humble and guards against overwhelming inflation and seductive illusion. All in all with this approach we abide with the Self, which bids each of us to walk a unique path of individuation.

Coming to a close, I would like to share some lines of poetry that I always keep in mind. The Swiss Gottfried Keller (1819-1890) writes, "Time . . . / is a caravansary, / We are the pilgrims within. . . ."[23] Likewise the thirteenth century Sufi mystic Rumi appeals to all wanderers, the "lover[s] of leaving:" "Ours is not a caravan of despair," he proclaims; "Come, even if you have broken your vows a thousand times."[24] Keller's "caravansary," Rumi's "caravan," and the *I Ching's* "stable base" can be seen as symbols of the Self or the ego-Self axis that steadily accompanies our sojourn. As in the Legend of the Wandering Jew, the poetic images point to inner *and* outer journeys—both of which belong to the path of individuation and spiritual development. Following this way as wandering pilgrims, we become better able to flexibly encounter the experiences of the road—whatever changes of habit are required, whatever new attitudes are demanded. The process of approaching the essence of the Self is indeed a never-ending trial and sojourn. The spirituality in pilgrimage is found by moving step-by-step.

NOTES

[1] I would like to thank Stacy Wirth, who in the course of editing came to share my interest in the topic, suggested several amplifications, and provided a number of references in English.

[2] St. James is known by many different names, depending on the language. For instance, in German he is St. Jakob, and in French, St. Jacques.

[3] Colline Serreau, writer and director, *St. Jacques ... La Mecque*; in English, *Start Walking* (Coproduction, France: Téléma, France 2 Cinéma, Eniloc Films, TPS Star, 2005).

[4] "'56, Sojourning, *Lü*,'" in "I Ching, The Classical Chinese Oracle of Change, The Divinatory Texts with Concordance," trans. Rudolf Ritsema and Stephen Karcher, in *Eranos 1993 - 1994 - 1995, Jahrbuch - Yearbook - Annales, Volume 62 - 64, Eranos, I Ching Project, Part I, 4-6* (Ascona: Eranos Foundation [no other date]), p. 596, original emphasis. Eds.' note: In large part, the interpretation and commentary in this version of the *I Ching* are given in single words and phrases (rather than prose); therefore, to avoid tedium, the forthcoming quotes are not endnoted; often paraphrased throughout, all are taken from scattered references to Hexagram 56, pp. 596-599.

[5] For what is widely regarded to be the seminal work, see George K. Anderson, *The Legend of the Wandering Jew* (Providence, RI: Brown University Press, 1965). See also for instance, Lovis M. Wambach, *Ahasver und Kafka: Zur Bedeutung der Judenfeindschaft in dessen Leben und Werk* (Heidelberg: Winter, 1993).

[6] Shelley Zer-Zion, "The Wanderer's Shoes, The Cobbler's Penalty: The Wandering Jew in Search of Salvation," in *Jews and Shoes*, ed. Edna Nahson, English Edition (Oxford: Berg, 2008), p. 143.

⁷ C.G. Jung, "V. The Type Problem in Poetry" [1921], in *Psychological Types, The Collected Works of C.G. Jung*, Vol. 6, § 454, eds. Sir Herbert Read, Michael Fordham, Gerhard Adler, William McGuire, trans. R.F.C. Hull, Bollingen Series XX, Ninth Printing, Rev. (Princeton, NJ: Princeton University Press, 1990). All subsequent references to the *Collected Works* will be by chapter title followed by volume and paragraph numbers.

⁸ See for instance, Roger of Wendover, *Flowers of History: The History of England from the Descent of the Saxons to A.D. 1265, Vol. II*, formerly ascribed to Matthew Paris, trans. J.A. Giles (London: Henry G. Bohn, M.DCC.XLIX), pp. 512-514, at *Internet Archive,* https://archive.org/details/rogerofwendovers02rogeiala (accessed 13 February, 2014).

⁹ Anonymous, "Kurtze beschreibung und Erzehlung / von einem Juden / mit Namen Ahasverus [1602]," in Urno Schmidt, *Das Volksbuch vom Ewigen Juden*, digital edition, Goethe Universität, Freimann-Sammlung Universitätsbibliothek UB (Danzig: Kafemann, 1927), pp. 5-8.

¹⁰ "Ahasverus" derives from an Old Persian name, linking the protagonist with the Persian King Ahasuerus (Xerxes), husband of the biblical Esther. Ahasuerus became the Jews' lauded advocate when he executed his prime minister for the crime of plotting to kill all the Jews in the kingdom. For a theory about the linkage of Ahasver[us] and the Persian king, and a connection with the Jewish Purim plays, see Aaron Schaffer, "The 'Ahasver-Volksbuch' of 1602," in *Modern Philology*, Vol. 17, No. 10, February, 1920 (Chicago: The University of Chicago Press), *JSTOR, Chicago Journals*, at http://www.jstor.org/stable/432928 (accessed 13 February, 2014).

¹¹ My compilation, summary, and modified translation, primarily with reference to Anonymous, *Kurtze Beschreibung*; Wendover, *Flowers of History*; Anderson, *The Legend*, and Wambach, *Ahasver*.

¹² Daniel J. Goldenhagen [1966], cited by Clemens Heni, "German Ideology: Understanding Ahasver, Mammon, and Moloch," in *Journal for the Study of Antisemitism (JSA)*, Volume 2, Issue 1, 2010, p. 53, at http://www.jsantisemitism.org/pdf/jsa_2-1.pdf (accessed 13 February, 2014).

[13] Tuvia Singer, "Interpretations of Wandering: The Discourses on the 'Wandering Jew' in the Fin de Siècle in Germany and Austria," in *From Collective Memories to Intercultural Exchanges*, ed. Marija Wakounig (Wien: LIT Verlag GmbH & Co. KG, 2012), p. 133.

[14] The Irish-born George Barrington (1744-1804) is generally attributed as the first recorder of the "Legend of the Flying Dutchman;" the story is well known through Richard Wagner's opera, *The Flying Dutchman*, originally, *Der Fliegende Holländer*, WWV 63 (1843).

[15] William Austin, "*Peter Rugg: The Missing Man*" [1824], in *Great Short Stories by American Writers*, ed. Thomas Fasano (Claremont, CA: Coyote Canyon Press, 2011).

[16] Zer-Zion, "The Wanderer's Shoes," pp. 141-142.

[17] See for instance the novel by Stefan Heym, *The Wandering Jew*, trans. Stefan Heym, European Classics, New Ed. (Evanston, IL: Evanston University Press, 1999).

[18] Marie Luise Kaschnitz, "Ahasver," in *Neue Gedichte* (Berlin: Claassen Verlag, 1957), p. 23, my translation.

[19] Deuteronomy 26:1-3 and 26:5, *Holy Bible,* Authorized King James Version, 9th Printing (Wheaton, IL: Tyndale House Publishers, 1987), original emphases.

[20] Jung, "The Psychology of the Child Archetype [1951]," Vol. 9i, § 291.

[21] Joan Chodorow, Dance Therapy and Depth Psychology: The Moving Imagination (New York: Routledge, 1991), p. 37.

[22] 2 Samuel, 6:16-17 and 6:20-22, *Holy Bible*, original emphases.

[23] Gottfried Keller, "Die Zeit geht nicht," in "Sonnwende und Entsagen," *Gesammelte Gedichte* [1883], Edition Holzinger Taschenbuch, Berliner Ausgabe, 2013 (North Charleston, USA: CreateSpace Independent Publishing, 2013), p. 115, my translation.

[24] Rumi, quoted in Roya R. Rad, *Rumi & Self Psychology (Psychology of Tranquility)*, trans. unknown (Victoria, VC, CA: Trafford Publishing, 2010), p. xi.

6

John Cage: Sound, Silence, Synchronicity

Craig E. Stephenson

To Austin Clarkson, musicologist, Jungian thinker, explorer of creativity in depth, with thanks for the loan of the tuning fork.

INTRODUCTION

The English poet, W. H. Auden, having taken up American citizenship in 1946, lived a good portion of the second half of his life in New York. In addition to writing poetry, Auden wrote hundreds of essays, reviews, introductions, and lectures. He also composed opera libretti. In an essay entitled "Some Reflections on Music and Opera," published in the *Partisan Review* in January-February 1952, Auden asks:

> What is music about? What, as Plato would say, does it 'imitate'? Choice. A succession of two musical notes is an act of choice, the first causes the second not in the scientific sense of making it occur necessarily, but in the historical sense of provoking it, of

providing it with a motive for occurring. A successful melody is
a self-determined history; it is freely what it intends to be, yet is
a meaningful whole, not an arbitrary succession of notes.[1]

At the same time that Auden was writing these reflections, and
not far from Auden's flat in Greenwich Village, John Cage was
composing *Music of Changes*. On January 1, 1952 at Judith Malina
and Julian Beck's Cherry Lane Theater, pianist David Tudor performed
this new work for the first time.

If we group Auden and Cage together not only in time and space
(New York City, 1952, although I can find no evidence that they ever
met) but also in aesthetics (both working their post-war ways out of
Romanticism and Modernism), and if we take up Auden's hypothesis
that music imitates choice, then we'll see just how provocative it was
for Cage to hand the choices to chance. Cage might rewrite Auden's
last sentence to read: "My composition, *Music of Changes*, is a chance-
determined history; it is freely what it intends to be (rather than
merely what I as composer intend it to be), yet it is a meaningful whole,
not an arbitrary succession of notes."

Whether or not a particular succession of notes becomes
"successful" depends very much on its listeners. Cage worked very hard
to highlight the role of listeners. As much as he composed, he educated
and provoked, preaching a radicalized receptivity to sound.

Historically, Jung's psychology plays a small part in Cage's oeuvre
because Jung's books and forewords to two books on Eastern religions
influenced Cage's artistic process. And so perhaps we can employ a
Jungian perspective as one way to understand and evaluate Cage's
aesthetic stance, as one way to approach listening to what Auden would
call the "meaningful whole" of Cage's work as he explores sound,
silence, and synchronicity.

PART 1: *MUSIC OF CHANGES* (1951)

John Cage was born in 1912 in Los Angeles. His father John Milton
Cage, Senior was a scientific inventor. His mother Lucretia had worked
as church pianist and journalist. Cage studied piano from the age of
eight. One biographer describes Cage the child as smart, sensitive, and
precociously inventive.[2] As an adolescent, he excelled at oratory, at
graduation he was class valedictorian, and although pious he was less
interested in his preacher grandfather's Methodist tradition and more

fascinated by the neighborhood Catholic Church's theatricality. After high school, Cage took a two-year stint in Europe to study music and architecture. He returned to the United States at the time of the Great Depression. He studied with the musical pioneer and pedagogue Henry Cowell and, on his recommendation, went to New York in 1934, where he survived on as little as twenty dollars a month, sleeping on a cot and washing the walls of the Brooklyn YWCA so that he could study with the modernist composer Adolph Weiss.

From 1935-37, Cage returned to Los Angeles to study with Arnold Schoenberg, the Austrian composer, famous for atonal music and his twelve-tone technique (and who had escaped the Nazis in 1933). Cage described his relationship with Schoenberg as creatively oppositional. Schoenberg goaded his students, saying "My purpose in teaching you is to make it impossible for you to write music," and Cage responded creatively to this provocation: "When he said that, I revolted, not against him, but against what he said. I determined then and there, more than ever before, to write music."[3] And Cage also defined himself against Schoenberg's twelve-tone system. With a fierce thinking logic, Schoenberg was arguing that in order to avoid privileging any one musical tone as dominant, all twelve tones in a row must be used before any could be repeated. Artists such as Kandinsky regarded the resulting dissonances as liberating music from neoclassicism, as releasing a spirituality inherent in art that had been trapped by conventional artistic schemas, thereby inspiring political and spiritual transformation in Western collective consciousness. But, as critic Kay Larson points out, as much as Schoenberg's work was historically audacious and liberating, his twelve-tone row is itself a closed system.[4] So Cage experienced Schoenberg both as a formidable instructor and an important opponent against whom he had to define his own values:

> When Schoenberg asked me whether I would devote my life to music, I said, "Of course." After I had been studying with him for two years, Schoenberg said, "In order to write music, you must have a feeling for harmony." I explained to him that I had no feeling for harmony. He then said that I would always encounter an obstacle, that it would be as though I came to a wall through which I could not pass. I said, "In that case I will devote my life to beating my head against that wall."[5]

Cage composed and performed percussion music, while employed at the Cornish School in Seattle and Mills College in San Francisco. Most of his compositions during the 1940s, commissioned for dance performances, were lyrical and minimalist and written for the prepared piano. Cage inserted screws, bolts, and other materials between the strings, transforming the piano into a percussion ensemble instrument under the control of a single player. Already he was defining music as the organizing of sound.

In the early 1940s, Cage moved to New York City at the invitation of art collector Peggy Guggenheim and her husband, the Surrealist painter Max Ernst (another recent immigrant escaped from arrest by the Gestapo in France). Cage stayed with them for a few weeks and then ended up for two months at the Greenwich Village apartment of dancer Jean Erdman and her husband Joseph Campbell. Cage composed for Erdman's dance performances, partly in exchange for his accommodation; for example, he describes *Ophelia*, 1946 as "a piece of dramatic character having a phraseology corresponding to that of the dance of Jean Erdman for which it was composed."[6] Campbell was publishing a book on Joyce's *Finnegan's Wake* in 1944 (a book that Cage returned to with his *Roaratorio* in 1979) and would soon publish *The Hero with a Thousand Faces* (in 1949). Cage worked on an opera (on the myth of Andromeda) with a libretto by Campbell, but the project was never completed. Erdman and Merce Cunningham, both dancers in Martha Graham's company, were working to free themselves from the narrative structures of her dance works. Graham was in Jungian analysis with Francis Wickes for many years and had grounded her art in Greek and American mythologies and framed her choreographic technique in a tension of opposites (physically, in the opposing movements of pelvic contracting and releasing). With Cunningham, Cage worked against psychoanalytic knowing and the privileging of meaning in the arts as much as against structural harmony.

In 1951, at age thirty-eight, rather than continuing to bang his head reactively in opposition to Schoenberg, Cage found a different approach. He was teaching Christian Wolff, a young musician and composer who had come to America in 1941 at the age of seven. Christian's parents had fled Nazi Germany; he had been born and raised in Nice, and the family escaped internment as enemy aliens during the Vichy regime. Cage, recalling his days as a penniless student and Schoenberg teaching him for free, took on Christian without pay. Christian's parents, Kurt Wolff and Helen Mosel Wolff, had been important publishers in Germany, and once settled in New York in 1942 they set up the publishing house, Pantheon Books, and eventually were invited to work on the Bollingen series. In 1951, having finished high school and preparing to leave on a reward trip to Europe, Christian, wishing to repay Cage, gave his teacher a copy of the newly published Bollingen edition of *The I Ching or The Book of Changes,* the Richard Wilhelm translation into German, the German rendered into English by Cary F. Baynes, with the foreword by Jung.[7] Following Jung's example, Cage began consulting the oracle for problems in his everyday life. But he also found the chart of the hexagrams in the appendices corresponded to his charts for composing, and so he methodically employed the oracle to generate numbers with which to determine pitch, duration, dynamics, and other aspects of composition, in order to create a music totally independent of his own tastes and preferences.

Cage began a new work, completed in four parts (May 16, August 2, October 18, December 13, 1951). He used the *I Ching* to determine the disposition of musical materials, to remove himself from the results and severe any connection between his personal tastes and his music. To select a sound, a duration, he would toss the coins, locate the number of its hexagram in the *I Ching,* then find the corresponding position on his charts. Every moment in his *Music of Changes* combined a chance-selected sound, including silences, time length, and loudness: "It is thus possible to make a musical composition the continuity of which is free from individual taste and memory (psychology) and also of the literature and 'traditions' of art." Cage was looking for a way to exclude artistic intention and ego from his composing. He invited chance rather than taste and individual invention to make the choices, leading towards an acceptance of sounds in their individuality, without the intrusion of a constraining will. In other words, as Cage stated, the charts gave him a first indication of the possibility of saying nothing.[8]

But these investigations were not nihilistic. For one thing, the scores are exquisitely designed, replete with invented notational images inked by hand. Neither were the performances improvisational. As pianist

Herbert Henck explains, the demands on the pianist were extreme: "The category of chance only plays a part at the moment of composition, but not at the moment of interpretation during the performance. The performer has to adhere strictly to a text of almost unprecedented exactness of notation."[9] Fortunately for Cage, the exceptionally talented pianist David Tudor accompanied him through the process of composing of *Music of Changes,* learning to play it as Cage composed it.

PART TWO: *4'33"* (1952)

Cage identified Aldous Huxley's 1945 book *The Perennial Philosophy*, with its fifteenth chapter entitled "Silence," as the source that first led him to Zen Buddhism.[10] He also mentioned an earlier influence, a 1936 lecture by Nancy Wilson Ross on "Dada and Zen Buddhism" during his time in Seattle.[11] In 1948, Cage read Jung's *The Integration of the Personality* (edited and translated by Stanley Dell) and found Jung's equivocal language useful for expressing an idea in a way that was valid both psychologically and spiritually.[12] From Jung, Cage formulated the notion that music could bring together the conscious and the unconscious and promote psychological wholeness:

> "I began to read Jung on the integration of the personality. There are two principal parts of each personality: the conscious mind and the unconscious, and these are split and dispersed, in most of us, in countless ways and directions. The function of music, like that of any other healthy occupation, is to help to bring those separate parts back together again. Music does this by providing a moment when, awareness of time and space being lost, the multiplicity of elements which make up an individual become integrated and he is one. This only happens if, in the presence of music, one does not allow oneself to fall into laziness or distraction... Neuroses act to stop and block. To be able to compose signifies the overcoming of these obstacles."[13]

A year later, in 1949, in the newly reprinted edition of Suzuki's *An Introduction to Zen Buddhism*, Cage would have read Jung's foreword (it was originally published as a foreword to the 1939 German edition but appeared in 1949 in English for the first time), although I've found no biography or essay that specifically mentions him reading this. Then, in 1951 Cage read Jung's foreword to the *I Ching*.

Around this time, Cage spoke of his intent "to compose a piece of uninterrupted silence and sell it to [the] Muzak Co. It will be 3 or 4 1/2 minutes long, those being the standard length of 'canned' music – and its title will be "Silent Prayer." It will open with a single idea which I will attempt to make as seductive as the color and shape and fragrance of a flower. The ending will approach imperceptibility."[14]

Cage was attending the classes of D. T. Suzuki at Columbia University. Suzuki had arrived in New York in 1950, settling there for six years, and lectured at Columbia, probably in March 1951. He was not a Zen master but a philosophical scholar of Zen who lectured internationally and published over thirty volumes. Suzuki was a cultural bridge-builder, comparing the sayings of Zen masters to the sermons of Meister Eckhart (his *Mysticism: Christian and Buddhist* would be published in 1957) and the American transcendentalists. And in his *Essays in Buddhism: Third Series,* Suzuki translates a dialogue and uses the word Unconscious (capitalized) as a way to describe Zen-mind: "The Unconscious is not describable as either existent or non-existent."[15] Likewise, describing the Flower Garland Sutra, Suzuki writes: "The sutras... are direct expressions of spiritual experiences; they contain intuitions gained by digging deeply into the abyss of the Unconscious, and they make no pretension of presenting these intuitions through the mediumship of the intellect."[16]

Cage would have found Jung highlighting precisely this bridging aspect of Suzuki's work, even if Jung's foreword came from the other direction (Jung's interest in Zen being most clearly expressed in his exchange of letters with Suzuki in 1933). Cage could read Jung drawing analogies between Meister Eckhart, Suzuki, and his own psychology:

> Satori corresponds in the Christian sphere to an experience of religious transformation... the mystic experience, which differs from other types (of religious experience) in that its preliminary stages consist in "letting oneself go," in "emptying oneself of images and ideas," as opposed to those religious experiences which, like the exercises of Ignatius Loyola, are based on the practice of envisaging sacred images. In this latter class I would include transformation through faith and prayer and through collective experience in Protestantism, since a very definite expectation plays the decisive role here, and not by any means "emptiness" or "freeness." The characteristically Eckhartian

assertion that "God is Nothingness" may well be incompatible in principle with the contemplation of the Passion, with faith and collective expectations. Thus the correspondence between satori and Western experience is limited to those few Christian mystics whose paradoxical statements skirt the edge of heterodoxy or actually overstep it. As we know it was this that drew down on Meister Eckhart's writings the condemnation of the Church. If Buddhism were a "Church" in our sense of the word, she would undoubtedly find Zen an insufferable nuisance. The reason for this is the extreme individualism of its methods, and also the iconoclastic attitude of many of the Masters.[17]

Cage did not take up Zen as a practice but stated that he came to approach his composing with Zen in mind. Already in the 1940s, he was describing composition in Jungian terms as an activity of integrating opposites, the rational and the irrational.[18] Cage told Suzuki that he would not practise *zazen* (i.e., sitting meditation), deciding "not to give up the writing of music and discipline my ego by sitting cross-legged but to find a means of writing music as strict with respect to my ego as sitting cross-legged."[19] Composing indeterminantly, sidestepping his composer ego's intentions by using the *I Ching*, exercising the discipline of throwing the three coins hundreds of time each day and submitting his musical creativity to the oracle, were his deliberate first steps in this direction.

The next step is famous. On August 29 1952, eight months after the premiere of *Music of Changes*, the first performance of John Cage's *4'33"* took place at the Maverick Concert Hall, an open-air theatre near Woodstock, New York. David Tudor sat down at the piano on the slightly elevated stage, opened the score before him, turned the pages, and kept time strictly with a stopwatch, closing the keyboard lid over the keys three times as he began each of the three movements of a composition in sonata form and raising the lid again at the end of the movements, timed at 30 seconds, two minutes 23 seconds, and one minute 40 seconds respectively (as determined by the *I Ching*).

4'33" was the second last piece in a benefit concert program of avant-garde music by the New York School of composers, Christian Wolff, Morton Feldman, Earle Brown, and Cage, as well as the French composer Pierre Boulez and Cage's first music teacher, Henry Cowell, all performed by David Tudor. For example, Henry Cowell's *The Banshee*, the final work of the evening, consisted entirely of noises derived from scraping the piano strings. But historically, it was the performance of *4'33"* that polarized the audience's responses. It became a turning point in Cage's life as well as in the history of twentieth-century music. As early as 1948, Cage had spoken of his intention to compose his "Silent Prayer." What, then, were the elements that pushed that intuitive statement of intent towards its realization four years later?

One element was Erik Satie, the French musician associated with the Dada movement, who became extremely important to Cage. Dada was the anti-art art movement that originated in Zürich in 1916. Rejecting bourgeois European culture that had plunged the world into war, the Dada artists dove into a nihilistic world of nonsensical art and plunged their audiences into chaos, randomness, and contradiction. (Jung said Dada was too idiotic to be called schizophrenic.[20]) In Satie's own time, Debussy and Ravel proclaimed him a Dadaesque precursor of modern music, and Cocteau praised him for finding in each new composition a renunciation. (Satie also composed for prepared piano before Cage, pieces of paper slid between strings to produce a straw-like wispy sonority.[21]) In July 1948, seeking to champion Satie's music when it was still dismissed as lightweight and idiosyncratic, Cage organized a Satie festival at Black Mountain College. In his lectures, Cage argued that, whereas Beethoven defined the parts of a composition by harmony, Satie defined them by time length:

> If you consider that sound is characterized by its pitch, its loudness, its timbre, and its duration, and that silence, which is the opposite and, therefore, the necessary partner of sound, is characterized only by its duration, you will be drawn to the conclusion that of the four characteristics of the material of music, duration, that is, time length, is the most fundamental. Silence cannot be heard in terms of pitch or harmony: it is heard in terms of time length. It took a Satie ... to rediscover this musical truth, which, by means of musicology, we learn was evident to some musicians in our Middle Ages, and to all musicians at all times... in the Orient. There can be no right making of music that does not structure itself from the very roots of sound and silence—lengths of time.[22]

The point being that no composer can structure harmonically for silence, but Cage could see that Satie structured his music for silence by composing instead from time lengths. Sparking much controversy, Cage's lectures were followed with a playful staging of Satie's one-act Dada comedy *The Ruse of Medusa* (a copy of which Cage had stumbled upon in the New York Public Library), cast with Buckminster Fuller as Medusa and Merce Cunningham as a monkey.

At this time, Cage's music itself was moving towards the theatrical, in that he was becoming interested as much in the relationship between performers and audiences as in composing. Anthropologist Victor Turner describes how attending a theatre performance or concert, like church-going, is for the most part a liminal experience: one emerges from the demarcated space and ritual time back into the profane with the collective cultural *imaginaire* re-affirmed. But Turner also identifies liminoid possibilities in theatrical performance, insofar as cultural standards may be religiously repeated and yet, at the same time, performatively subverted.[23] Cage worked with Julian Beck and Judith Malina and the Living Theatre company in their experiments inspired by Antonin Artaud's manifesto in *The Theatre and Its Double*. It's not surprising, then, to find Cage experimenting with the roles of performer and audience, even reversing the roles in *4'33"*, so that the performer takes up the silent role, and the audience "acts" by listening differently, at the very least by becoming conscious, perhaps even critical, of its shared expectation that the performance should reaffirm a common belief.

How did the audience at the outdoor Maverick Concert Hall respond to the reversing of roles that night, as David Tudor closed and opened the keyboard lid three times? In the end, we know many members responded angrily, but it would be interesting to know what happened during the performance. It has been suggested, for instance, that *4'33"* put an artistic frame around American environmental sounds, creating a moment—à la Marcel Duchamp—for the audience to listen to how the American environment sounded. This is not so far-fetched. Cage was very fond of Thoreau and could have aligned his "Silent Prayer" composition easily with the mandate of the American transcendentalists who argued that, in order to paint a native landscape that did not look like Europe, one had to start over, grounding oneself in a North American aesthetic. In order to compose or listen to music that did not sound like Europe, one had to begin again by listening to where one was. The audience in the outdoor hall that evening found itself in the midst of a New England soundscape:

> And when one reads the Zen texts attentively, one cannot escape the impression that, however bizarre, satori is a natural occurrence, something so very simple, even, that one fails to see the wood for the trees, and in attempting to explain it invariably says the very thing that throws others into the greatest confusion...When the Master asks, "Do you hear the murmuring of the brook?" he obviously means something quite different from ordinary "hearing."[24]

This isn't Cage, it's Jung writing about Suzuki who draws analogies between Zen and American transcendentalism.

But there are more possible layers of significance to *4'33"*. A few months before the first performance, as a resident teacher at Black Mountain College, Cage produced a multi-media musical event entitled *Theater Piece No. 1*, grounded in Artaud's aesthetic argument that all the elements of theatre can be viewed independently: sound, movement, music, lights, words may all operate equally, with no one element, such as text, dominant over the others. In *Theater Piece No. 1*, Cage had his performers playing in precise chance-determined lengths of time, within a mise-en-scène of all-white paintings by Robert Rauschenberg, suspended at various angles. It was a carefully timed and structured example of indeterminacy, a pre-sixties Happening: Cage reading Meister Eckhart from a ladder, Rauschenberg playing Edith Piaf records, Cunningham and his dancers moving through the four audience spaces, and Tudor playing the piano. Again, *Theater Piece No. 1* was not improvisational, it was the simultaneous presentation of these independent elements in a space in such a way that the audience could synthesize them, could experience synchronistic moments emerging from the surface chaos, feel the sudden aligning of resonances and perhaps even of meaning. In "Lecture on Nothing," Cage describes this kind of open-ended receptivity: "As we go along / (who knows) / an i-dea may occur in this / talk. I have no idea / whether one will / or not. / If one does / let it. Re /gard it as something / seen / momentarily, / as / though / from a window / while traveling."[25]

We know *Theater Piece No. 1* was not merely a Dada performance (in Jung's understanding of Dada as idiotic) because Cage was framing these compositions in Zen language. And in a letter, the young Rauschenberg described his 1951 white paintings employed in the mise-en-scène as numinous, using words steeped in a religious connotation:

> They are large white (1 white as 1 God) canvases organized and selected with the experience of time and presented with the innocence of a virgin. Dealing with the suspense, excitement and body of an organic silence, the restriction and freedom of absence, the plastic fullness of nothing, the point a circle begins and ends. They are a natural response to the current pressures of the faithless and a promoter of intuitional optimism.[26]

For Cage, these paintings were a revelation: he stated explicitly that they gave him the courage to compose *4'33"*. He wrote: "To Whom It May Concern: The white paintings came first; my silent piece came later."[27]

So, the first performance of *4'33"* evoked a space not only for the natural surround but also for its inherent numinosity. Around the same time as *Theater Piece No. 1* (1951/1952), Cage visited one of two anechoic chambers at Harvard University. The room was insulated with acoustically absorptive material to eliminate echoes and outside noise. Once alone inside, he heard two sounds, one high and one low. He asked the sound engineer about these. The engineer, not at all surprised, identified the high sound as Cage's nervous system operating, the low as his blood circulating. Cage reports his conclusion in his "Lecture on Something:" "No silence exists that is not pregnant with sound."[28] And from this conclusion, Cage's mind began to leap forward, to consider the implications if silence was not the opposite of sound:

> I had honestly and naively thought that some actual silence existed. So I had not really thought about the question of silence. I had not really put silence to the test. I had never looked into its impossibility. So when I went into that sound-proof room, I really expected to hear nothing. With no idea of what nothing could sound like. The instant I heard myself producing two sounds, my blood circulating and my nervous system in operation, I was stupefied.[29]

After this experience, Cage stopped schematizing sound and silence as a pair of opposites. He would describe their relationship differently: silence is to sound as zen-mind or Unconscious or Jungian self is to ego. The one is the ground for the other; it subsumes and surpasses the other.

This accumulation of philosophical, artistic, and personal forces moved Cage in one direction, the composition and performance of *4'33"*. It was not an ironic prank, even though it may have been designed to be paradoxical, to subvert rationality—by composing silence. Musicologist and composer Kyle Gann, who has brilliantly catalogued all these vectors converging in Cage's life and more, in his book, *No Such Thing As Silence*, wonders if Cage was attempting to trigger in the audience a right-brain experience with which he was familiar as a composer.[30] But Gann's idea overlooks the fact that David Tudor performed explicitly the marking of the passage of time with a stop-watch and the turning of pages. It would perhaps be more correct to say that Cage was attempting to trigger a whole-brain experience, or what Mihaly Csikszentmihalyi (1990) calls "flow," directing awareness in order to experience consciously the mind in optimal connectedness.[31]

Of course, there also exists the possibility in Cage's intention for something shadowy, in his case perhaps pious and preachy from his Methodist grandfather that may have secretly delighted in pushing his audience's faces into the silence, into Nothingness. This could also account for some of the anger sparked that night in the Maverick Concert Hall.

But one final anecdote sheds light and lightness on this piece that Cage considered the most important of his oeuvre. It is a personal memory that Cage recalled at age 70 (and it's my favorite story from this research on Cage at this moment in my life). In 1940, the music section of the Works Projects Administration (a make-work program first instituted by F.D. Roosevelt in 1935) would not admit Cage as a musician because he played percussion instruments; that is to say, some bureaucrat decided that a percussionist is not really a musician. Cage was eventually reclassified as a recreation leader and could only be employed by the WPA recreation department. His first assignment was to go to the hospital in San Francisco and entertain the children of the visitors, but he was not allowed to make any sounds doing this, for fear of disturbing the patients. So he organized games for the children that involved moving around rooms and counting, creating silent rhythms in time-space.[32] This reminds us to keep in mind Cage's playful inventiveness.

PART THREE: *SILENCE* (1961)

At age forty-nine, Cage's life changed dramatically with the publication of a collection of his lectures and writings, entitled *Silence*. John Rockwell of the *New York Times* has described the book as "the most influential conduit of Oriental thought and religious ideas into the artistic vanguard—not just in music but in dance, art and poetry as well."[33]

PART FOUR: *0'00"* (*4'33"* No. 2, 1962)

Cage's composition *0'0"* consists entirely of the following instructions:

> Solo to be performed in any way by anyone. In a situation provided with maximum amplification (no feedback), perform a disciplined action. Four stipulations: The piece may be performed with any interruptions and will focus on "fulfilling in whole or part an obligation to others." No two performances may repeat the same action, nor may they create a "musical" composition. And there should be no emphasis on "the situation (electronic, musical, theatrical)."[34]

Cage composed *0'00"* while touring Japan for the first time. He visited Suzuki and then wrote his composition to zero. Previously Cage had worked to free up composition, but the demands on the performer were extreme, *4'33"* being indeterminate in its composition but determinate for the performer. Now *0'00"* became indeterminate in both. Cage wrote:

> Though no two performances of the *Music of Changes* will be identical...two performances will resemble one another closely.... The function of the performer in the case of the *Music of Changes* is that of a contractor who, following an architect's blueprint, constructs a building. That the *Music of Changes* was composed by means of chance operations identifies the composer with no matter what eventuality. But that its notation is in all respects determinate does not permit the performer any such

identification: his work is specifically laid out before him. He is therefore not able to perform from his own center but must identify himself insofar as possible with the center of the work as written. The *Music of Changes* is an object more inhuman than human, since chance operations brought it into being. The fact that these things that constitute it, though only sounds, have come together to control a human being, the performer, gives the work its alarming aspect of a Frankenstein monster.[35]

Clearly, by 1962 the composer of *Music of Changes* had moved on. The problem was that performers needed to value the responsibilities begat from the freedom being offered by Cage as composer. The 1991 production of *Europeras 1 & 2* at the Zürich Opera was a scandalous case in point. The performance led Cage to write an angry letter of protest, accusing the musicians of causing deliberately its failure. Musicologist and Jungian scholar Austin Clarkson evaluates that performance and its aftermath in his article, "The Intent of the Musical Moment: Cage and the Transpersonal."[36] He observes that experiential music was not in the Zürich musicians' repertoire, and Cage had not understood the challenges he was placing on them. Clarkson argues that if the orchestra had consisted all of David Tudors, then the performance could have constellated in the moment a kind of collective *satori* for the musicians and audience together. Clarkson knew Tudor personally and attests: "Tudor's phenomenal powers as an executant and his devotion in realizing and performing indeterminate scores are legendary. What marked Tudor's approach, aside from his musical gifts, was his openness to the transpersonal." And when Clarkson asked Tudor how he thought the Zürich performance could have been improved, Tudor replied: "It would have been better if they were more fully aware that they are all individuals."[37] Clarkson concludes that, for Cage, the individual musician is not egoistic, willful, and ethically uncommitted to the enterprise. The individual musician's actions arise not only from the ego but also from the guiding center of the personality, the source of ethical impulses that link the individual to society. Cage put this more succinctly: "Everything I have composed since 1952 was written for David Tudor."[38]

Cage's *0'00"* defined a music of actions that do not have predictable outcomes. Clarkson emphasizes the challenge implicit in its directions: "If the musical content were reduced to a minimum and the outcome stripped of expectations, the performer would be open to the spontaneous flow of the imagination, and performing music would be a creative rather than a re-creative act."[39] Taking up this challenge, Clarkson worked with music students at Canada's York University, helping them perform creatively rather than recreatively, presentationally rather than representationally. He notes that if the schema was too loose, the musician had too much freedom and the imagination was not sufficiently engaged. If the schema was too tightly controlled, the response was not spontaneous enough, and the musical imagination had too little scope. For Clarkson, the fear on the part of academics and performers that experimental music seeks the destruction of composed music can be assuaged when presentational and representational states are understood as complementary.

Cage wasn't interested in improvisation if, like free association, it leads merely to the cathartic re-expression of habitual patterns. Neither was Cage's creative pragmatism conceptualist. On performing Satie's *Vexations*, a fifty-two beat motif to be repeated 840 times, Cage wrote:

> In the middle of those eighteen hours of performance, our lives changed. We were dumbfounded, because something was happening which we had not considered and which we were a thousand miles away from being able to foresee. So, if I apply this observation to conceptual art, it seems to me that the difficulty with this type of art, if I understand it correctly, is that it obliges us to imagine that we know something BEFORE that something has happened. That is difficult, since the experience itself is always different from what you thought about it. And it seems to me that the experiences each person can have, that everyone is capable of appreciating, are precisely those experiences that contribute to changing us and, particularly, to changing our preconceptions.[40]

Performed as conceptualist art, *4'33"* would render silence merely banal. Performed as a presentational and liminoid work that deconcentrates attention in an attempt to change preconceptions, *4'33"* is understandably Cage's most important work and fundamental to his entire oeuvre. David Tudor argued that it can be one of the most intense listening experiences one can have.

CONCLUSIONS

Cage opens *Silence* with a provocation, a manifesto on music (written for Judith Malina and Julian Beck and the Living Theater): "Nothing is accomplished by writing a piece of music."[41] His Greenwich Village neighbor Auden wrote: "Poetry makes nothing happen."[42] In response to Schoenberg, Cage went looking for freedom from harmony, to sensitize listeners to the spirituality inherent in noise, to sound as the primary sensation.

Cage the provocateur of the avant-garde New York movement of the early fifties, in the context of that time, made a space for sounds to be heard which were not harmonious, not musical in the conventional sense, certainly not expected. In doing so, he pointed to the reality that sound is continuous but often unnoticed, under-appreciated. Reading Cage as he reads Jung confirms what Clarkson so astutely identifies as the transpersonal context to his composing.

The neuroscientist and musician Seth Horowitz argues that in the evolution of vertebrates, there are no deaf animals. All animals with backbones hear (although there are plenty of blind animals or animals with a limited sense of smell or touch), and hearing is the most universal of all senses:

> Vision is a relatively fast-acting sense that works slightly faster than our conscious recognition of what we see. Smell and taste are slowpokes, working over the course of seconds or more. Touch, a mechanosensory sense, can work quickly (as in light touch) or slowly (as in pain), but only over a restricted range. By contrast, animals and humans can detect and respond to changes in sounds that occur in less than a millionth of a second and to the content of complex sounds over the course of hours. Any detectable vibration represents information, to be used or ignored. And in that simple concept lies the entire realm of sound and mind.[43]

Thinking back to Cage's experience of hearing his neural synapses and blood vessels operating in the Harvard anechoic chamber, I'm sure he would be intrigued to learn from Horowitz that at the top of spectrum of sound is the 9,192,631,770 cycles per second of an energized cesium-133 atom, and at the bottom of the spectrum is the sound of black holes, characterized not by silence but a B flat 57 octaves below middle C.

NOTES

[1] W. H. Auden, "Some Reflections on Music and Opera," *Partisan Review*, January-February 1952, in *The Complete Works of W. H. Auden, Prose*, Volume 3, 1949-1955, ed. Edward Mendelson (Princeton: Princeton University Press, 2008), p. 296.

[2] Kenneth Silverman, *Begin Again: A Biography of John Cage* (Evanston, Illinois: Northwestern University Press, 2010), p. 5.

[3] Kay Larson, *Where The Heart Beats: John Cage, Zen Buddhism, and the Inner Life of Artists* (New York: Penguin, 2012), p. 55.

[4] *Ibid.*, p. 57.

[5] John Cage, "Indeterminacy," in *Silence* (1961, Middleton: Wesleyan University Press, 2011), p. 261.

[6] Cage, "Ophelia," 1946, in *Piano Works 1935-48*, Piano Solo (London: C. F. Peters Corporation, Henmar Press, 1977), pp. 36-48.

[7] Richard Wilhelm, trans., *The I Ching or Book of Changes*, Bollingen Series XIX, Cary F. Baynes, trans., German to English (1950, Princeton, Princeton University Press: 1950/1981).

[8] Cage, "Composition: To Describe the Process of Composition Used in *Music of Changes* and *Imaginary Landscape*," in *Silence*, pp. 57-60.

[9] Herbert Henck, "Notes," in *John Cage, Music of Changes* (1951), Herbert Henck, Piano (Wergo Records, CD 1982/1988), p. 13.

[10] Richard Kostelanetz, *Conversing with Cage* (1988, New York: Limelight Editions, 1988/1994), p. 254.

[11] David W. Patterson, "Cage and Asia: History and Sources," in *The Cambridge Companion to John Cage*, ed. David Nicholls (Cambridge: Cambridge University Press, 2002), p. 43. See also Kyle Gann, *No Such Thing as Silence: John Cage's 4'33"* (New Haven: Yale University Press, 2010), p. xiii.

[12] Cage, "A Composer's Confessions," Address before the National Inter-Collegiate Arts Conference, Vassar College, 1948, in *Musicworks*, vol. 52, Spring 1992, pp. 6-15. See also Craig Stephenson, "Reading Jung's Equivocal Language," in *Possession: Jung's Comparative Anatomy of the Psyche* (London: Routledge, 2009), pp. 99-120.

[13] Cage, "A Composer's Confessions," in *Musicworks*, pp. 6-15.

[14] Larson, *Where The Heart Beats*, p. 139.

[15] Daisetz Teitaro Suzuki, *Essays in Zen Buddhism: Third Series*, ed. Christmas Humphreys (1953, New York: Samuel Weiser, 1953/1971), pp. 35-37.

[16] *Ibid.*, p. 22.

[17] C. G. Jung, "Foreword to Suzuki's *Introduction to Zen Buddhism*" (1939), in *Psychology and Religion: West and East, The Collected Works of C. G. Jung*, eds. Sir Herbert Read, Michael Fordham, Gerhard Adler, William McGuire, trans. R.F.C. Hull (Princeton: Princeton University Press, 1969), Vol. 11, §§ 893-894. Hereafter reference to Jung's *Collected Works* follows by chapter title, volume number, and paragraph number.

[18] Larson, *Where The Heart Beats*, p. 356.

[19] Cage, "Tokyo Lecture and Three Mesostics," *Perspectives of New Music*, vol. 26, no. 1, Winter 1988, p. 7. See also Gann, *No Such Thing*, p. 138.

[20] Jung, "The Role of the Unconscious" (1918), CW 10, § 44.

[21] Nicolas Southon, "Erik Satie," in *Erik Satie: Avant-dernières pensées*, Harmonia Mundi S.A., CD 2009, pp. 19-20.

[22] Cage, "Defence Defense of Satie," in ed. Richard Kostelanetz, *Conversing with Cage* (New York: Limelight Editions, 1988), pp. 81-2, in Gann, *No Such Thing as Silence*, p. 80. See also Cage, "Erik Satie," in *Silence*, pp. 76-82.

[23] Victor Turner, *From Ritual to Theatre: The Human Seriousness of Play* (New York: Performing Arts Journal Publications, 1982), p. 33.

[24] Jung, "Foreword to Suzuki's *Introduction to Zen Buddhism*" (1939), CW 11, §§ 884, 891.

[25] Cage, "Lecture on Nothing," in *Silence*, p. 110.

[26] Robert Rauschenberg, "Letter to Betty Parsons, 18 October 1951," in Larson, *Where The Heart Beats*, p. 234.

[27] Cage, "On Robert Rauschenberg, Artist, and His Work," in *Silence*, p. 98.

[28] Cage, "Lecture on Something," in *Silence*, p. 135.

[29] Cage, *For the Birds*, ed. Daniel Charles (Boston: Boyars, 1981), pp. 115-116.

[30] Kyle Gann, "No Escape from Heaven: John Cage as Father Figure," in *The Cambridge Companion to John Cage*, ed. David Nicholls (Cambridge: Cambridge University Press, 2002), pp. 242-260.

[31] Mihaly Csikszentmihalyi, *Flow: The Psychology of Optimal Experience* (New York: Harper, 1990).

[32] Cage, "After Antiquity," in Kyle Gann, *No Such Thing as Silence: John Cage's 4'33"* (New Haven: Yale University Press, 2010), p. 59.

[33] John Rockwell, "Classical View: Cage Merely an Inventor? Not a Chance," *The New York Times*, August 23, 1992.

[34] Larson, *Where the Heart Beats*, pp. 377-383.

[35] Cage, "Composition as Process: II. Indeterminacy," in *Silence*, p. 36.

[36] Austin Clarkson, "The Intent of the Musical Moment: Cage and the Transpersonal," in *Writings Through John Cage's Music, Poetry and Art*, eds. David W. Bernstein and Christopher Hatch (Chicago: Chicago University Press, 2001), pp. 62-112.

[37] *Ibid.*, p. 74.

[38] Cage, *For the Birds*, p. 120.

[39] Clarkson, "The Intent of the Musical Moment," p. 66.

[40] Cage, *For the Birds*, pp. 153-154.

[41] Cage, *Silence* (1961, Middletown: Wesleyan University Press, 2011), p. xxxii.

[42] W. H. Auden, "In Memory of W. B. Yeats," in *Another Time* (New York: Random House, 1940).

[43] Seth Horowitz, *The Universal Sense: How Hearing Shapes the Mind* (London: Bloomsbury, 2012), p. 4.

7

Shameful Hush
Breaking the
Conspiracy of Silence

Lucienne Marguerat

Silences. Not the silences between notes of music, or the silences of a sleeping animal, or the calm of a glassy surfaced river witnessing the outstretched wings of a heron. Not the silence of an emptied mind. But this other silence. That silence which can feel like a scream, in which there is no peace. The grim silence between two lovers who are quarreling. The painful silence of the one with tears in her eyes who will not cry. The cry of the child who knows she will not be heard. The silence of a whole people who have been massacred. Of a whole sex made mute, or not educated in speech. The silence of a mind afraid to admit the truth to itself. This is the silence the poet dreads.[1]

—*Susan Griffin*

S witzerland's *Verdingkinder*, our so-called "contract children," were hushed for more than one hundred years before their dire straights became a matter of public debate starting in the early 1980s. Only then would the truth gradually emerge: Starting in the early nineteenth century, and until the 1970s, they were the hundreds of thousands of "surplus or unwanted" children, the "discarded" ones, who worked under the auspices of foster care as indentured child laborers.[2] Whether voluntarily given up by the parents or coercively removed, these children were handed over by state authorities to fulfill needs for cheap labor on farms. Into the 1930s, many children came to this plight by public auction. Most were brutally flogged, many sexually abused and submitted to other heinous treatment. The *Verdingkinder*—literally, the "children made into things"—are the subjects of a painful and sad chapter in Swiss history. This is the chapter on a coercive welfare system veiled by "the silence the poet dreads," to borrow from Susan Griffin.

SILENCE: A FORM OF VIOLENCE

Silence can eat into body and soul, as it did for the majority of contract children whose numbers increased in the rural areas of Switzerland from around the mid-nineteenth century onward. Not only did silence surround the abusive practice of child labor as such. Not only was silence imposed on the children's suffering of further unspeakable abuses. The equal violence, perhaps even greater one, was the silence inflicted in the form of the government's prolonged refusal to acknowledge and stop these practices, to apologize, and to support a healing process. Until reparative measures were set into motion, the survivors were scattered far and wide, little known or linked to one another, much less known to the Swiss public at large.

The first to break the taboo, in 1924, was Carl Albert Loosli (1887-1959), himself a former foster child raised in an institutional home.[3] Most exceptionally among the survivors, he would become one of Switzerland's most respected intellectuals and renowned authors. To my best knowledge, Loosli's works have yet to be translated in English. For many years his autobiographical books and articles made of him a lone fighter for the cause. Later, in the 1940s, a few small changes at local levels were brought about thanks to the biographies of other former contract children;[4] by articles on the maltreatment of children in educational institutions;[5] and by reports on the sexual abuse of a foster boy.[6] Contributing to the shut down of one institutional home, Paul Senn's photographs illustrated reports that were published in 1944 by the journalist Peter Hirsch under the pseudonym Peter Surava.[7]

Verdingkind [1], Canton Bern, 1940 (Photo by Paul Senn)

In 1949 a lone guardian's protest set off an investigation of sadistic practices enacted on children in a religious institutional home in Canton Lucerne.[8] Yet nothing much changed until the 1960s, with further published testimonies about coercive practices in the provision of social welfare.[9] Critical reports continued to increase until 1978.

Only then did foster care become regulated by new law, which made the placement of contract children illegal.

Many more years would pass before the final breakthrough. Not until 2009—thirty-one years after the adoption of the new law—did the story of the contract children become exposed to a wider public, namely with the touring exhibition *Stolen Childhood, Contract Children Speak*.[10] In 2004, professional associations and scholars began to lobby the federal government to finance research on a national scale, the purpose being to develop plans for restitution and to improve the regulation of foster care. In the same year a nationally supported research project called for the testimony of all former contract children. Between April 2005 and March 2008, two hundred fifty survivors were interviewed.[11] Now the taboo was definitely broken, the conspiracy of silence came to an end. With great relief these adult survivors discovered they were not alone, they shared in the suffering of similar hardships and trauma, they had no more reason to be isolated in feelings of shame and guilt. But these two hundred fifty are the mere few.

Recent records suggest that today in Switzerland, at least 10,000 survivors—now adults ranging from about sixty to ninety years old—remain uncontacted or off the record. Many have confessed privately that they still feel too ashamed to speak up. All the respondents willing to be interviewed expressed a pressing need to speak out before they die, both for their own sakes and for the sake of contract children whose lives were destroyed by suicide, drug abuse, psychiatric treatment, or criminality. Most of them re-live the pain of their childhood ordeal as they watch their own grandchildren growing up in loving families. They all sought healing, welcomed the prospect of official apology, and hoped for financial compensation for the damage done—and they wish their testimony to prevent forever the repetition of such injustice to children.

In 2009 a member of the Swiss Federal Council unveiled the previously mentioned exhibition, *Stolen Childhood, Contract Children Speak*, which featured recordings of adult survivors talking about their experiences from 1920-1960. Touring the country for nearly three years, the exhibit overlapped the 2011 premiere of the movie, *The Foster Boy (Der Verdingbub)*, a docudrama set in the 1950s, which has by now gained international acclaim.[12] On April 11, 2013 a memorial

Verdingkind [2], Canton Bern, 1940 (Photo by Paul Senn)

day was held for all victims of coercive welfare. The Federal Council now publically apologized for the past practices and permitted abuses, which included also compulsory abortion, sterilization, confinement in psychiatric clinics, and the jailing of victims without trial. An ombudsperson was appointed and hotlines opened in all cantons. A project was launched to collect and analyze historical data on a national scale. In January 2014 the Federal Council announced the creation of a victims' fund with CHF seven to eight million to be furnished by private donors as well as cantons and communes. In addition, a "solidarity fund" has been established to take care of cases in need of urgent material support.

"I Have Never Been A Somebody"

The personal histories emerge as nightmares. The average foster child was traumatized from the start by forced separation from his or her birth family, typically done without warning or explanation. Infants as well as older children were torn from their mothers' arms, crying and kicking. Others were tricked, being promised a fun outing. Still others were picked up directly from school by strangers and brought to unknown places, for unknown reasons. Most if not all of them were subsequently placed on Swiss farms, supposedly for foster care. These children, some already at the age of four, were forced to daily labor before dawn and soon became overworked, sleep-deprived, hungry, and malnourished. Many had no choice but to continue with chores throughout the day—for instance arising to carry milk to the dairy, returning home to a meager breakfast, then walking the long way to school, only to return home again to work over lunchtime, and then walk all the way back to school. When school was over, they returned home immediately to take up other chores. There was little if any time for their attention to homework for school—let alone time to recover from illness or injury. The priority was labor—and to be clear, it was unpaid.

There are plentiful accounts of children receiving daily floggings with the likes of leather straps, wooden shoes, cast iron pans. Many of them, both girls and boys, were sexually abused by their foster fathers or both parents, or by a foster brother, or a farm hand. Forbidden to reveal to outsiders the events of such "family life," the rare child nevertheless dared to break the taboo, seeking the help of a minister, physician, teacher, or policeman. However such a child rarely reached out again, discovering that the supposed advocates were more persuaded by the foster families' denials—and finding him- or herself thrashed more severely than ever for speaking out.

The children endured the silence of withheld dialogue, hearing only commands with humiliations that sunk deep into their souls: "Your own family is worthless and so are you;" "you and your kind are good for nothing;" "your family is genetically deficient;" "you are nothing and nothing will ever come of you, so don't bother with wishing." Most of them were entirely shut out of their foster family's lives and homes. They slept with animals in unheated sheds. What little food was provided, they were forced to eat alone. Most often,

Verdingkind with His Foster Father, Canton Bern, 1946 (Photo by
Paul Senn)[13]

the contract children were not only kept away from their biological
families, but were also unable to learn where their kin lived. Very rarely,
short visits by an aunt or uncle, father or mother might have been
permitted. The occasional gift brought along—a coat, a pair of shoes,
a little money, a watch—was immediately seized for the foster family's
own use. But children who came to this "foster care" as babies or in
early childhood knew nothing at all about their origins, and would
discover them, if ever, only in adulthood. So the only family and home
they knew was the place of their ordeal.

Pre-announced visits by state guardians, usually once a year,
were deceptions conducted as show. The contract child was bathed

and dressed up ahead of time, and a family bedroom inside the house was pretended to be his or her own. If a state guardian questioned the child at all, then it was always in the presence of the foster parents, and the child knew full well how to respond: "Everything is fine." Yet these children arrived at school typically late (due to the priority of work), raggedly dressed, filthy, stinking, heads full of lice. School provided safety and refuge only for the few who managed to perform well, thereby gaining their teachers' affections. The majority however found in their schools yet one more friendless place, a place of constant discrimination, humiliation, unjust punishment, and mockery.

Research in the area of parent/child bonding has long established the tragic outcomes of an environment that deprives a child of emotional security and continuity of care. Not surprisingly then, many contract children were severely impaired in their human relationships and cognitive abilities, and were therefore likely to fail at school. Almost none of them continued schooling beyond the compulsory age of fifteen. Very few undertook low paid professional apprenticeship, as was and still is the custom in Switzerland for many young people. Economy was certainly a factor. But the main reason was, contract children were held to be unworthy of advancing their lives. Barely educated and with no other practical skills, most continued to serve as farm hands or do other labor up to, if not beyond, the age of twenty (the age of legal adulthood at the time).

In adulthood some survivors made the difficult decision to try to regain their lost identity, aiming to discover why they had been removed from their biological families in the first place, and what had become of their kin. Some wanted to learn why, as contract children, they were so easily replaced and moved from one farm to another. The state authorities threw obstacles in their paths, sometimes denying them access to their files until lawyers intervened. Or they were forbidden to make copies of their documents, a procedure that blocked release of the legal proof of their treatment. Many found that their files had been destroyed. The obstructions gave rise to great disappointment, bitterness, and ultimately to general mistrust in society.

"All my life I had to learn how to be," says one survivor; "you were not allowed to exist, you had no one. I got no love from anyone." Although knowing about the abuses, neighbors, teachers, clergy, the police, and other potential advocates usually looked away. Sometimes a farmer's wife would sneak an apple into a small hand, but that was about the extent of communal empathy. The feelings of helplessness and inferiority were overwhelming. One survivor put it in a nutshell: "I have never been a somebody."[14]

HOW HAVE THEY SURVIVED?

To be fair, a few former contract children report the good fortune of lives lived with genuinely caring foster parents. Some felt rescued from the poverty, neglect, or abuses of their birth families. But others rebelled, fleeing to nearby relatives, seeking brief shelter before journeying on to another hopefully better place. Most who fled were found and returned to their foster families. Some suffered a temporary loss of speech, evidencing psychological dissociation as a means to survive overwhelming trauma. Nearly all of them became passive and withdrawn. As one survivor explains, "When you are flogged all the time, you go numb. You stop protesting, you say nothing about your pain."

The most dreadful aspect of the ordeal, say the survivors, was not the violence, or the hunger, or the hard labor. The worst thing was the lack of love—bodily contact saved only for brutal beatings and sexual abuse, words saved only for reprimand, threat, and humiliation. Living in constant fear, with no hope of improvement or escape, many remember passivity and resignation being the only ways to withstand their treatment as sub-human outcasts. The research thus far has been unable to determine how many committed suicide.

Miraculously, a number of contract children managed to retain an inner resilience. Of these, some survivors mention the comfort they gained from animals—the cows that kept them warm, the faithful farm dogs and cats, the reliable workhorse. Some found solace in the hope of the rare visits with relatives, or of secret meetings with kin on the way to school. A few discovered soul nourishment in their schools, this being the only place where they felt safe and free. Some found soothing in religious faith. Some took flight in imagination, gaining comfort in secret inner companions. Some enjoyed sharing secrets with a foster brother or sister. For at least one, music came to the rescue. Yet the survivors know their wounds will never heal entirely and that they will always feel somehow "different."

Many survivors—to this day undereducated and impaired in human relationships—are unable to sustain employment, friendships, marriage, and adequate parenting. These are the socially isolated, the lonely and mute, in their souls still traumatized, split and dissociated, suffering chronic anxiety, depression, compulsion. Some describe the strain of silently bearing their ordeal, of being secretly plagued by overwhelming guilt and self-loathing while raising their own children. Others try to tell their stories in intimate circles, only to find themselves met with disbelief or lack of understanding. For some, decades pass before memories flood in spontaneously; only after retirement may they begin for the first time to reveal to their spouses and children the endured atrocities.

As two hundred and fifty life stories were collected between 2005 and 2008, historians took note that a process of reparation had finally begun.[15] It was discovered that the sharing of personal story is a step toward healing, offering survivors the chance to re-live consciously and with adequate containment the enduring trauma, pain, and shame. Imbuing past experience with continuity and meaning, the process also offered the chance to consolidate lost or damaged identities. However, the organized efforts toward reparation revealed that apology and healing are not achieved solely with the sharing and collection of victims' histories. These stories, historians came to realize, constitute but one side of the history and one truth. A genuine effort to heal would have to strive for a comprehensive picture, one that would integrate *other* truths and realities. The aim as such amounted to what could be called psychic integration on a collective level. It would entail also the effort to let go of a reassuring line that put the "good" victims on one side and the "bad" perpetrators on the other. To fail to let go of this line would be to deny the perspective of the perpetrators, they themselves being victims of the era's politics, economy, social mores, and religious convictions.

OTHER REALITIES, OTHER TRUTHS

Among the realities and truths belonging to the healing process would be those of the state authorities who were charged to deal with social welfare cases. Unfortunately, the representatives of the authorities involved were all deceased before the official process of reparation got underway. Their unfound records were presumably destroyed, if not for overt purposes of obfuscation, then by the legal means that permit the destruction of records after ten years. However, scholars have helped to retrieve their voices by an examination of history, summarized as follows:

As a fledging federal democracy and nascent welfare state at the turn of the century, Switzerland had only just begun to create measures for the care of the needy. In 1912 the law permitted child labor; indeed it was self-evident that children of the lower classes would work, as was the case elsewhere in the world. Financial aid for severely impoverished families was virtually unknown. Typically, "surplus children" were surrendered or claimed by the state, and the communities paid "maintenance fees" to foster parents and institutions. All the more so were foster children committed to work. The law provided for the forcible removal of children from their homes when none other than the state welfare authorities themselves deemed it necessary for the health and moral education of the children. Legal grounds for such coercive action were, for instance:

- family conditions of destitute poverty;
- family conditions of "depravity"—including among others parental alcoholism, unwed mothers, a minor's illegitimate pregnancy;
- familial abandonment, i.e. by one or both parents due to divorce, disabling illness, or death.

Lying behind the coercive practices was the socio-religious estimation of poverty as a self-inflicted condition, and accordingly, the belief that extremely poor parents were morally deficient and incapable of raising children. Similarly the law furthered the perception that social stability originates in the orderly family, with clearly defined gender roles: the father at the head, able in body and mind—the mother a support for husband and children. Thus, all foster children were assigned state guardians who were given the task of organizing their care. These guardians were responsible for ensuring that the children would grow up under healthy conditions, receiving sound moral and practical education. While many children were sent to institutional homes, farmers were held to be the ideal foster parents, not last because farm work was conceived to be the best source of education. Finally, the state guardians were charged to monitor the children's well being up to the age of legal adulthood, at the time, twenty years old.

It is crucial to note that professional welfare administration and social work had not yet come into being. So the state authorities, including the guardians, were laymen. They all lived in small, tight-knit rural communities, whose inhabitants were personally familiar with one another, and survived in mutual dependence—both socially and economically. At the time, and decades thereafter, Switzerland was by no means the prosperous nation it is today. The average citizen struggled to make a living, the farmers in particular. To remain with this example, the farmers were in dire need of farm hands, whom they could ill afford to pay. Under the circumstances, the spirit of charity intended in coercive welfare degenerated in practice to chattel trade with obvious advantages for the dealers: Most often forcibly removed from home, the foster children were sometimes sold at auction. Many state guardians received or kept kickback payments for their placement services. Farmers and others obtained cheap labor. The foster families and institutional homes economized by withholding material care, thus making profit off their maintenance fees. Finally, the communities, seemingly oblivious to the actual practice, rested assured that their moral and financial responsibilities for the poor were absolved. In Jungian terms we could say that all involved, trying to survive, became victims of a collective shadow.

Evolution Of Childrearing

It should be helpful to put the social welfare practices and plight of the contract children into the context of the evolution of childrearing in general. As the American psychoanalyst and psychohistorian Lloyd deMause observed in 1974,

> The history of childhood is a nightmare from which we have only recently begun to awaken. The further back in history one goes, the more likely children are to be killed, abandoned, beaten, terrorized, and sexually abused.[16]

In fact, from ancient times and into the nineteenth century children were commonly treated as objects. This was the case even though, as deMause maintains, "true empathy" in childrearing started to emerge during the sixteenth century, in what he calls the "intrusive mode."[17] Due to "'. . . improvement in the level of care and reduced mortality,'" upper class families were now freer to invest more in their children's growth and emotional well-being; and with this, they wanted "'only to control [the children] . . . and make [them] 'obedient.'"[18] To this end, it was acceptable and common to keep children in check with threat, humiliation, shaming, and deception. DeMause sees a strong rise of psychological empathy in the eighteenth century, which would correspond with the Enlightenment and its conception of childhood as a distinct phase of life. Thus,

> [t]he socializing mode of childrearing that began in the eighteenth century and that continues to be the ideal of most nations today . . . replaced . . . absolute obedience . . . with parental manipulation and psychological punishments, in order to make the child "fit into the world" as a replica of the parent.[19]

The child-rearing practices "of each age [or era]," deMause posits, aim to "reduc[e] adult anxiety. . . ."[20] In what we could call an archetypal approach, he explains the origin of this defense to lie in "spontaneous" psychological processes, which are common to "successive generations," and "independent of social and technological change." As children "strive" toward relationship with their parents and other caretakers, the adults naturally regress, experiencing themselves at the "psychic age" of the children. In this ordinarily healthy regression toward an experience of mutuality, adults with childhood trauma tend to unconsciously fear the child, who threatens to re-constellate the ordeal. In such cases, regressive methods of childrearing defensively keep the child at bay.

With deMause's ideas in mind, we can posit that, well into the 1970s, the rural enclaves of Switzerland were influenced by the collective unconscious in their management of children in general. For into the twentieth century, their handling of the contract children themselves involved practices that deMause links with pre-antiquity, antiquity, and early Christianity: forced fosterage and child labor; terrorization by sexual abuse; and abandonment by exclusion from the family, by deprivation of adequate food, shelter, and clothing, and by child-swapping. If their own children weren't routinely subjected to all such practices, they were nevertheless required to labor, and were typically disciplined with harsh methods that point back to the sixteenth century. In contrast, Swiss urbanites participated largely in the evolution of new values, including those that bring increasing empathy to childrearing.

In fact, the world of the Swiss farmer does differ from the world of the Swiss urbanite, as it always has. Moreover, our farmers—constituting one of the nation's most powerful conservative lobbies—take fierce pride in their difference. Let us assume that to embody this pride and identity is to have been raised in such an unrelenting manner, and possibly to have witnessed the sub-human treatment of contract children in one's own family. In this case, the tormenting of the contract children for decades under the guise of childrearing would be somewhat understandable. It would furthermore follow the familiar pattern by which the perpetrator tends to re-enact upon others the traumatizing behavior that was perpetrated upon him/herself.

Whose Fault Was It?

The facts of this history suggest that too many decision makers were deaf to "the children weeping . . ." as the poet Elizabeth Barrett Browning wrote in 1844; "They are weeping . . . In the country of the free."[21] As far back as that time, Browning shed light on the predicament of forced child labor in industrial England. In 1978 Swiss federal law finally demanded an end to child labor and called for improved regulation of foster care. Yet *five years* passed before the law was finally implemented. And now, recent reports tell us that a number of educational institutions have continued to exploit foster children, often under the guise of religious obedience. Another dark chapter of Swiss history slowly comes to light. I feel compelled to ask: how can such abuse continue in my country? After all, we Swiss take great pride in being citizens of one of the world's most highly developed democracies and guardians of human rights. For all the soul-searching and reparation we have undertaken, we have neglected as a collective to look into our misdoings.

I recall the seminal work published in 1967 by the German psychoanalysts Alexander and Margarete Mitscherlich: *Inability to Mourn: Principles of Collective Behavior.*[22] The Mitscherlich's book—far ahead of the prevailing Zeitgeist—triggered Germany's coming-to-terms with the Holocaust and its aftermath. The Mitscherlichs held that, collectively, the Germans had taken false comfort in blaming the unspeakable atrocities solely on Hitler and his henchmen. Dissociated from the evil and overwhelming feelings

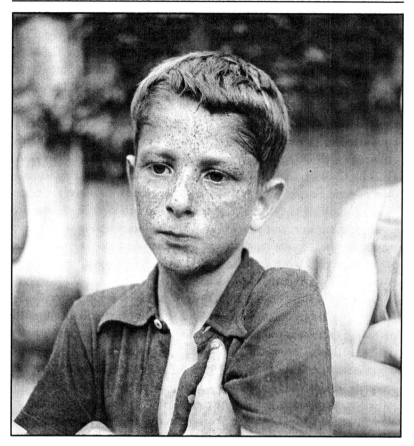

Orphan Boy, Institutional Home Sonnenberg, Kriens 1944 (Photo
by Paul Senn)[23]

of guilt, shame, and grief, the Germans were caught in narcissistic
denial and complacency about the past, choosing instead to invest
in the future. What had allowed them to develop this defensive
strategy, say the Mitscherlis, were the rigid norms and values of
the 1920s and 1930s, which encouraged the projection of repressed
shame and other ill feelings onto the Jews (and eventually onto
homosexuals, Gypsies, and all others deemed to be devious,
immoral, etc.). Only by taking back the projections, by releasing
repressed feelings, and by learning to discern personal prejudice,
would it be possible to adequately mourn, and thus, too, to avert
future enactments of such evil.

To return by analogy to the process of reparation in Switzerland: As the government in 2013 finally acknowledged and apologized for the wrongdoings and later agreed to financial compensation for the victims, the historians themselves had already asserted the guilt of the state welfare authorities. All sides concur that the state guardians themselves—entrusted by law to protect the foster children—neglected to question their trustees confidentially, and neglected to intervene for the sake of the children's well being. Moreover, they always announced their home visits in advance, allowing the foster parents to stage the appearance of a normal family life. When they moved the children from one place to another, they apparently saw no need to explain the reasons. Shutting their eyes to the witnessed abuses and keeping silent about what they heard, the guardians appear to have actively sought to collude with foster families, institutional homes, and others entrusted with the children's care.

As deMause puts it in relationship to child rearing specifically: "Only by reducing dissociation to a minimum through empathic parenting can we avoid inflicting the self-destructive power we now have available to us."[24] Similarly, Alexander and Margarete Mitscherlich pled for education that trains mature, critical egos. In a Jungian perspective, this would all be part and parcel of the individuation process. C.G. Jung himself was wary of the seductiveness of unconscious identification with collective beliefs, projections and denials. In his view, the task of the ego is less a daily fight with our inner demons—for such a fight can never be won. It is rather to come to terms with our own dark sides and to develop a sense of wholeness and trust, beyond one's inevitable personal inner tensions.

Jung attributed another factor to the upsurge of collective violence: the tremendous power of archetypal symbols on the psyche. The deepest psychic layers (the collective unconscious) that within each of us respond to symbols, Jung explained, know no morals. The implication is that our reactions can go either way—toward violence, or toward a release of love and creativity. However, Jung rejected the notion that we can control our destructive urges by reason alone. He warned on the contrary not to overestimate the capacities of the rational ego. The only hope in his view was for as many people as possible to accomplish the task of individuation, which implies the need to open up to and watch closely for the influence of insidiously ascending collective ideas.

Thus, at the end of the day, the responsibility for the violation of civil rights lies with each of us, individually. Applied to the history of contract children in Switzerland, a collective healing will have to involve all sides—not only victims and representatives of the authorities, but the larger public as well. The atrocities of the past cannot be undone. However, we all have the possibility to learn and admit our own disquieting potential to enact the worst. With this insight grows the awareness of our own connectedness with all beings on earth. In my view, this is the best remedy against systematic abuse and social exclusion.

NOTES

[1] Susan Griffin, "Thoughts on Writing: A Diary," in *The Writer on Her Work*, ed. Janet Sternberg (New York: W.W. Norton and Company, 1980), p. 117.

[2] Kim Wilsher, "No One Could Help Me Escape," in *The Telegraph*, 14 March 2004, at http://www.telegraph.co.uk/news/worldnews/europe/switzerland/1456838/No-one-could-help-me-escape.html (accessed 9 April, 2014). See also, Isabelle Eichenberger, "A Dark Chapter in History: Recognising Switzerland's 'Slave Children,'" trans. Sophie Douez, in *SWI swissinfo.com*, August 9, 2013, at http://www.swissinfo.ch/eng/swiss_news/Recognising_Switzerland _s_slave_children.html?cid=35429120 (accessed 9 April, 2014).

[3] Carl Albert Loosli, *Anstaltsleben. Werke Band I* (Zürich: Rotpunktverlag, 2006).

[4] See for example, Ernst Fischer, *Vom Verdingbub zum Strafuntersuchungsrichter: Aus meinem Leben* (Affoltern a.A.: s.n., 1946); Walter Hottiger, *Der Verdingbub: Erzählung* (Basel: Reinhardt, 1942); and Siegfried Joss, *Sämi: Schicksal eines Verdingbuben* (Basel: Reinhardt, 1949).

[5] Peter Hirsch, "Ein gewisser Joseph Brunner," in *Er nannte sich Peter Surava* (Stäfa: Rothenhäusler Verlag, 1991).

[6] Hirsch, "Nur ein Verdingbub," in *Er nannte sich.*

[7] All photos reproduced in this essay are by Paul Senn (1901-1953), with the permission of FFV, Kunstmuseum Bern, Dep. GKS, © GKS.

[8] Martina Ackermann, Markus Furrer, Sabine Jenzer, *Bericht Kinderheime im Kanton Luzern im Zeitraum von 1930-1970* (Luzern: Gesundheits- und Sozialdepartement des Kantons Luzern, 2012), p. 68.

[9] See for example, E.R., "Ich war im Heim. Erschütternder Tatsachenbericht," *Soziale Schriftenreihe des Landesverbandes freier Schweizer Arbeiter, H38* (Flawil: 1963); and Gottfried Keller-Güntert, *Ein Verdingbub oder: Gibt es einen Gott? Ein Lebensbild* (Andelfingen: Thur-Verlag, 1969).

[10] See *Enfances volées | Verdingkinder reden* at http://www.enfances-volees.ch (accessed 13 April, 2014). See also Imogen Foulkes, "Swiss Contract Children Speak Out," in *BBC News Europe* at http://www.bbc.co.uk/news/world-europe-16620597 (accessed November 20, 2013).

[11] These interviews took place in the context of the research project, "Verdingkinder, Schwabenkinder, spazzacamini und andere Formen der Fremdplazierung und Kinderarbeit in der Schweiz im 19. und 20. Jahrhundert," 2005-2008, *Aktionsgemeinschaft Verdingkinder*, at http://www.verdingkinder.ch/projekte.html (accessed 13 April, 2014).

[12] Markus Imboden, director, *Der Verdingbub | The Foster Boy* (Global Screen GmbH, 2011). See also Foulkes, "Swiss Contract Children," in *BBC News.*

[13] My translation of the original photo caption, *Verdingknabe mit seinem Pflegevater, Kanton Bern, 1946.*

[14] Marco Leuenberger, Loretta Seglias, eds., *Versorgt und vergessen. Ehemalige Verdingkinder erzählen* (Zürich: Rotpunktverlag, 2008). Author's note: quotes from the survivors in the foregoing and forthcoming paragraphs are scattered throughout the cited source, my translations. See also for example, Lotty Wohlwend, Arthur Honegger, *Gestohlene Seelen. Verdingkinder in der Schweiz* (Frauenfeld: Verlag Huber, 2004).

[15] See the report in Heiko Haumann, Ueli Mäder, "Erinnern und Erzählen" in Leuenberger and Seglias.

[16] Lloyd deMause, "The Evolution of Childhood," in *History of Childhood: The Untold History of Child Abuse*, Lloyd deMause, ed. (New York: Harper & Row, 1974), p. 1.

[17] deMause, "The Evolution of the Psyche and Society, Chapter 9" in *The Emotional Life of Nations*, at *Lloyd deMause and Psychohistory*, www.psychohistory.com/htm/eln09_psychesociety.html (no page numbers, accessed 15 April, 2014).

[18] Ibid.

[19] Ibid.

[20] Ibid., "Childhood and Cultural Evolution, Chapter 7," in *The Emotional Life of Nations*, at http://www.psychohistory.com/htm/eln07_evolution.html (accessed 15 April, 2014).

[21] Elizabeth Barrett Browning, "From Poems (1844), I" in *Elizabeth Barrett Browning: Selected Poems*, eds. Marjorie Stone, Beverley Taylor (Ontario: Broadview Press, 2009), p. 151.

[22] Alexander Mitscherlich, Margarete Mitscherlich, *Inability to Mourn: Principles of Collective Behavior*, 2nd Ed. (NY: Grove Press, 1984). For the original German see, *Die Unfähigkeit zu trauern: Grundlagen kollektiven Verhaltens* (München: Piper & Co, 1967).

[23] My translation of the original photo caption, *Heimknabe, Erziehungsanstalt Sonnenberg, Kriens, 1944.*

[24] deMause, "The Evolution of the Psyche," in *The Emotional Life of Nations*.

8

Synopsis: Rowing for Tranquility in Times of Burnout

Ingela Romare

Rowing (Still by Ingela Romare from *Rowing for Tranquility*, 2010)

T he topic of the Jungian Odyssey 2013—*Echoes of Silence: Listening to Self, Soul, Other*—suggested a fitting context in which to offer a viewing of my film, *Rowing for Tranquility in Times of Burnout*.[1] I was inspired initially by Bodil Stefansson's very moving book, *Roddkraft (The Power of Rowing)*, which lays bare the author's personal experience of near burnout.[2] As a number of patients in my psychotherapy practice were presenting with the condition, I contacted Bodil, hoping to hear more of her thoughts on the matter. She responded with an invitation for me to go rowing at sea with her, which we did several times, in spring, summer, fall, and winter. The film quietly relays the story of Bodil's healing journey, as shared during our trips together in her little rowboat, she at the helm with the oars and I in the stern with my camera.

Bodil Stefansson (Still by Ingela Romare from *Rowing for Tranquility*, 2010)

And so we learn about Bodil's recovery, with its inner and outer dimensions. Just when she felt most exhausted, empty, and lost, an inner voice said, "I want to row!" Deciding to heed it, Bodil bought a little boat, one small enough to handle by herself and big enough for rowing safely into the open ocean. She began to row throughout the whole year, through all seasons and weather. Ritually repeating these outings, she discovered in the silence of being alone at sea the possibility to open up and *listen*. She listened to her heart and to her Self. She listened to the wind, the water, and the animals around her—the Others on her journey. She encountered nature outside and within herself. Little by little this fundamental, essential experience renewed her life balance and energy, and led her to face her life with new insights and courage.

NOTES

[1] Ingela Romare, director, *Rowing for Tranquility in Times of Burnout*, in the original Swedish, *Ro i utbrändhetens tid* (Myt & Bild, 2010); for more information visit www.ingelaromare.se (in Swedish only). The film (55 min.) with English subtitles is available on DVD and may be purchased on request. Write to Ingela Romare at romare@mbox301.swipnet.se or Hanneborgsvägen 62, 26978 Torekov, Sweden.

[2] Bodil Stefansson, *Roddkraft: att göra det man verkligen vill* (Stockholm: Wahlström & Widstrand, 2004).

9

Synopsis: Listening to the Unconscious—Listening to the Ancestors, About the Archetypal Roots of Jungian Psychology

Peter Ammann

My lecture at this Jungian Odyssey offered the audience the chance to listen for or attune to the primordial indigenous roots of C.G. Jung's Analytical Psychology, in particular their African ones. The affinities between Jungian psychology and African Traditional Healing seem to prove the basic fact that Jung's concepts are not artificially or purely intellectually conceived constructions, but correspond with our direct perception of psychic life. In other words, Jungian concepts have a natural basis in the way humans beings have been and still are experiencing their psyche, consciously or unconsciously, across cultures, and from time immemorial until today.

To illustrate, I drew on several sources, beginning with my personal experiences and research in South Africa, which includes the

testimonies of African Traditional Healers (especially Dr. Nokuzola
Mndende and Charmaine Joseph). Another essential source is the
groundbreaking book by the South African Jungian pioneer Vera
Bührmann: *Living in Two Worlds, Communication Between a White
Healer and Her Black Counterparts.*[1] Last but not least, I showed
excerpts from three films that document my research and invite
the viewers to witness African Traditional Healers and Bushmen
healers, both in dialogue and during their performance of healing
rituals. Readers of this synopsis can view excerpts at my website:
Healing in Two Worlds . . .;[2] *Spirits of the Rocks* (on the Bushpeople
and their rock paintings);[3] and *Living in Two Worlds . . . Vera Bührmann.
Interview by Mario Schiess.*[4]

Dr. Nokuzola Mndende at the IAAP Congress Cape Town 2007 (Still by
Peter Ammann from his film, *Healing in Two Worlds . . .,* 2008)

As Jung himself held, "[T]he unconscious corresponds to the
mythic land of the dead, the land of the ancestors."[5] The resources
that we explored lay bare this correspondence and the "African seeds"
or early precursors to some other important Jungian concepts. To cite
but a few examples, in a nutshell:

> • The African healers reveal that the Jungian
> personal unconscious corresponds with those
> African ancestors "whose faces we know" (parents,
> grandparents, family, friends, etc.)—while the

Charmaine Joseph, In Durban (Photo by Jane Bedford, 2009)

Jungian collective unconscious corresponds with the African ancestors "whose faces we don't know."

Bushpeople (San), A Healing Trance Dance (Still by Peter Ammann from his film, *Spirits of the Rocks,* 2002)

• A most striking correlation between Jungian psychology and African Traditional Healing emerges in their common recognition of the crucial role that dreams play both in training and therapy. For Jungians the dream is an a priori reflection of and guide to the unconscious and its messages; hence our attunement to dreams is a central concern of training and analytic treatment. For African healers important dreams are messages from the ancestors, and as such they are the most significant guideline during their training and later practice with clients.

• Another parallel lies in the distinction between "great dreams" and "ordinary dreams." In Jungian parlance the great, archetypal dreams arise from and illuminate meanings from the collective unconscious, while more ordinary dreams reveal the personal unconscious. For the African Traditional Healers the great dreams, in contrast to ordinary dreams, are special revelations from the ancestors.

• The Jungian practice of active imagination as a means of contacting the unconscious is consistent with the African practice of listening to, dialoguing, and negotiating with the ancestors.

• The psychic energies that Jungians recognize, resonating for instance in the transference and countertransference, are present and concretely embodied by the African healers. As Vera Bührmann put it, "They act out what we talk about."

• The Jungian concepts of anima and animus find their concrete counterparts among certain African ethnic groups, who represent what they call their "spirit spouses" in form of carved feminine and masculine sculptures.

Whilst staking a claim for the rootedness of Jungian psychology in the African indigenous cultures, I'm aware that these roots can be found also in indigenous cultures of other continents. However, according to the most widely accepted Out-of-Africa theory, all indigenous cultures in the end derive from the African continent, rightly called the cradle of humanity.[6]

NOTES

[1] Vera Bührmann, *Living in Two Worlds, Communication Between a White Healer and her Black Counterparts* (Pretoria: Human and Rousseau Ltd., 1984).

[2] Peter Ammann, producer and director, in collaboration with Georg Schönbächler, *Healing in Two Worlds—Jungian Psychotherapists Encounter African Traditional Healers*, film documenting the panel discussion and workshops at the XVII International Congress for Analytical Psychology IAAP, Cape Town 2007 (© Peter Ammann,

2008). Excerpts of this and my other documentaries can be viewed at www.peter-ammann.ch, where the DVDs are available for purchase.

[3] Peter Ammann, director, *Spirits of the Rocks* (Zürich: Triluna Film AG, 2002).

[4] Peter Ammann, director, *Living in Two Worlds: Communication Between a White Healer and her Black Counterparts—Vera Bührmann: Interview by Mario Schiess* (© Peter Ammann, 2007).

[5] C.G. Jung, *Memories, Dreams, Reflections*, ed. Anelia Jaffé, trans. Richard and Clara Winston, Rev. Ed. (New York: Vintage, 1989), p. 191.

[6] For an overview of, and resources on, the Out-of-Africa theory, see, "Recent African Origin of Modern Humans," *Wikipedia, the Free Encyclopedia*, at http://en.wikipedia.org/wiki/Recent_African_origin _of_modern_humans (accessed 17 April, 2014).

About AGAP, ISAPZURICH, and the Jungian Odyssey

A GAP, the Association of Graduate Analytical Psychologists, was founded as a Swiss-domiciled professional association in 1954 by the American Mary Briner and several other international graduates of the C.G. Jung Institute Zürich. AGAP is a founding member of the International Association for Analytical Psychology (IAAP, 1955). In 2004, AGAP delegated its IAAP training right to a sub-group of some ninety members who in turn founded the International School of Analytical Psychology Zürich (ISAPZURICH). Thus, since 2004, ISAPZURICH has been conducting postgraduate training in Analytical Psychology under the auspice of AGAP.

Since 2006 the Jungian Odyssey has taken place each semester as an off-campus week-long retreat, open not only to the students of ISAPZURICH, but also to all with interest in C.G. Jung. In keeping with the Homeric journey, the Odyssey travels from year to year, finding "harbor" in different Swiss "ports." A hallmark of the Jungian Odyssey is its thematic inspiration from the *genius loci*, the spirit of the place, to which it travels from year to year.

ISAPZURICH was honored to begin collaborating with Spring Journal Books in 2008, when Nancy Cater proposed the publication of an annual series based upon each year's Odyssey lectures. The inaugural volume, *Intimacy: Venturing the Ambiguities of the Heart*, was published in 2009, ensuing from the Jungian Odyssey 2008.

The Jungian Odyssey
Annual Conference and Retreat   Venue   JO Series

		Venue	JO Series
2006	Jungian Psychology Today: Traditions and Innovations & The Quest for Vision in a Troubled World: Exploring the Healing Dimensions of Religious Experience	Flüeli-Ranft	
2007	Exploring the Other Side: The Reality of Soul in a World of Prescribed Meanings	Gersau	
2008	Intimacy: Venturing the Uncertainties of the Heart	Beatenberg	Vol. I, 2009
2009	Destruction and Creation: Facing the Ambiguities of Power	Sils Maria	Vol. II, 2010
2010	Trust and Betrayal: Dawnings of Consciousness	Gersau	Vol. III, 2011
2011	The Playful Psyche: Entering Chaos, Coincidence, Creation	Monte Verità	Vol. IV, 2012
2012	Love: Traversing Its Peaks and Valleys	Flüeli-Ranft	Vol. V, 2013
2013	Echoes of Silence: Listening to Soul, Self, Other	Kartause Ittingen	Vol. VI, 2014
2014	The Crucible of Failure	Grindelwald	*Forthcoming* Vol. VII, 2015

All published volumes of the Jungian Odyssey Series can be
ordered online at www.springjournalandbooks.com.

Editors

Series Editors

Ursula Wirtz, PhD, Academic Chair of the Jungian Odyssey, is a training analyst and graduate of the C.G. Jung Institute Zürich (1982), maintaining her private analytical practice in Zürich. She received her doctorate in philosophy from the University of Munich and her degree in clinical and anthropological psychology from the University of Zürich. She has taught at a number of European universities, and authored numerous publications on trauma, ethics, and spirituality, translated into Russian and Czech. She has lectured worldwide and taught at various European universities. Her forthcoming book, *Trauma and Beyond: The Mystery of Transformation,* will be published in the Zürich Lecture Series in Analytical Psychology by Spring Journal Books, 2014. She is a faculty member of ISAPZURICH, and a trainer with developing Jungian groups in Eastern Europe.

Stacy Wirth, MA, born in North Carolina (1954), has lived in Switzerland since 1979, when she joined the man who would become her Swiss husband. At the time she carried on her previous work as a dancer and choreographer, and went on to raise two daughters. In the interim she received her MA in the psychology of art from Antioch University (1997), and completed her training at the C.G. Jung Institute Zürich (2003). From 2004-2010 she served on the AGAP Executive Committee. She is a co-founder and training analyst of ISAPZURICH, a member of the Advisory Board of *Spring Journal*, and a Jungian analyst with a private practice in Zürich.

Deborah Egger, MSW, is a training, supervising and founding analyst of ISAPZURICH with private practice in Stäfa. Born in Little Rock, Arkansas, she moved to Zürich in 1986 to train at the C.G. Jung Institute in Küsnacht, and remained in Switzerland having met her husband here. They raised two children and various animals (cats, turtles, rabbits, guinea pigs and a dog named Twinkle!). She was

President of AGAP for nine years, in this role serving also for six years as a member of the Executive Committee of the International Association for Analytical Psychology (IAAP). Her BA degree is in Religion and Psychology and she holds an MSW in clinical social work. Her analytic areas of focus are in adult development and relationships and transference.

Katy Remark, PhD, received her diploma from the C.G. Jung Institute in 2003 and is now a member of ISAPZURICH. Besides working as an analyst, she is also a Certified EMDR Therapist, a Certified Imago Relationship Therapist, and has studied and trained in body-centered psychotherapy. Her professional interests include the use of visualization and the somatic pathway in working with assertiveness, anger, aggression, and panic. She maintains a private practice in Zürich.

Consulting Editor

Nancy Cater, JD, PhD, is the editor (since 2003) of *Spring: A Journal of Archetype and Culture*, the oldest Jungian psychology journal in the world, and the author of *Electra: Tracing a Feminine Myth through the Western Imagination*. She is the publisher of Spring Journal Books, which specializes in publications by leading scholars in depth psychology, the humanities, and cultural studies. She is an Affiliate Member of the Inter-Regional Society of Jungian Analysts, a former appellate court attorney, and lives in New Orleans, Louisiana.

Contributors

Peter Ammann, Dr. phil., studied music (cello) and graduated from the University of Zürich in musicology, ethnology, and history of religion. Encouraged by Jung himself, as well as by his own personal analysts Jolande Jacobi and Marie-Louise von Franz, Peter later trained at the C.G. Jung Institute Zürich. He is now a training analyst, supervisor, and lecturer at ISAPZURICH, maintaining private practices in Zürich and Geneva. He is equally an awarded filmmaker who, after completing an apprenticeship as assistant to Frederico Fellini on *Satyricon*, focused on documentary work and the integration of a Jungian perspective in his own films. His 1984 encounter with Laurence van der Post ignited his enduring interest in South Africa, the Bushpeople and their rock paintings, and African Traditional Healing. Among his many documentaries are, *Hlonipa: Journey into Wilderness*; *Sandplay with Dora Kalff*; *Spirits of the Rocks*; and most recently, *Mabi's Feast—Sangomas Celebrating San*. Peter's lecture tours take him regularly to Switzerland, the UK, the US, and South Africa.

Lionel Corbett, MD, trained in medicine and psychiatry in England and as a Jungian analyst at the C.G. Jung Institute of Chicago. His primary interests are: the religious function of the psyche, especially the way in which personal religious experience is relevant to individual psychology; the development of psychotherapy as a spiritual practice; and the interface of Jungian psychology and contemporary psychoanalytic thought. Dr. Corbett is a core faculty member of Pacifica Graduate Institute in Santa Barbara, California, where he teaches depth psychology. He is the author of numerous professional papers and three books: *Psyche and the Sacred*; *The Religious Function of the Psyche*; and *The Sacred Cauldron: Psychotherapy as a Spiritual Practice*.

Allan Guggenbühl, Prof. Dr. phil., received his degrees in education and psychology from the University of Zürich, and in 1994 earned a diploma from the C.G. Jung Institute Zürich. He is a training analyst at ISAPZURICH, and editor of the German-language Jungian journal *Gorgo*. He is also the founder and director of the Institute for Conflict Management in Bern, which has disseminated his methods of mythodrama and crisis intervention in Swiss schools, among other places. His publications in English include the book, *Men, Power and Myths: The Quest for Male Identity*, trans. Gary Hartman (Continuum, 1997); and the essays, "Love: Our Most Cherished Anarchist—or Path to Failure?" (2009), and "Self-Betrayal: A Psychological Necessity?" (2011), published in the *Jungian Odyssey Series*, respectively Vols. I and III (Spring Journal Books).

Waltraut Körner, lic. theol., received her degree in theology from the University of Zürich. She is a training analyst at the C.G. Jung Institute Zürich, Küsnacht, and maintains a private practice in Zürich. The topic addressed in her unpublished thesis, "Die Rolle des Animus bei der Befreiung der Frau" ("The Animus and His Role in Women's Liberation"), still engages her. The depth psychological background of anti-Semitism is also among her longstanding and current interests. She has held several public lectures on this theme and published the article, "The Wandering Jew," in *Eranos Yearbook 1997: Gateways to Identity, Vol. 66*, eds. James G. Donat, Jay Livernois (New Haven, CT: Spring Publications, 1999); published in German as, "Ahasver—der ewige Wanderer: Eine Archetypische Schattenfigur," in *Analytische Psychologie, Band 29, No. 1, 1998*, Hrsg. H. Diekmann (Basel: Karger, 1998). Over the years she has translated Jungian literature from English to German, especially works by Marie-Louise von Franz, and also C.G. Jung's *Die Psychologie des Kundalini-Yoga: Nach Aufzeichnungen des Seminars 1932*, Hrsg. Sonu Shamdasani (Olten, Switzerland: Walter Verlag, 1998).

Lucienne Marguerat, lic. phil., was born in 1943 in Lausanne, Switzerland. She graduated with a degree in sociology from the University of Geneva. She moved to Zürich and worked as an IT specialist for twenty years, before completing the training in analytical psychology at the C.G. Jung Institute Zürich. She has a private practice in Zürich and is actively involved as a trainer at the International School for Analytical Psychology (ISAPZURICH). She has been lecturing and writing on various topics including picture interpretation, *Art Brut* or Outsider Art, the creative process, time, and the impact of collective projections on the individual psyche.

Dariane Pictet, AdvDipExPsych, received her degree in Comparative Religion from Columbia University. A graduate of the C.G. Jung Institute Zürich, Küsnacht, she serves as a Training Analyst with ISAPZURICH and also with the London groups, the Guild of Analytical Psychology (GAP), and the Independent Group of Analytical Psychologists (IGAP). Her previous lectures on comparative mysticism have been published in the *Jungian Odyssey Series,* Vols. I, II, and V. She delights in poetry and practices yoga.

Jo Ann Hansen Rasch is a New Zealand-born and American educated writer living in Switzerland. Her previous poetic contribution to the Jungian Odyssey Series, "To Nietzsche," appeared in Vol. II, *Destruction and Creation: Facing the Ambiguities of Power.* Her poems, short stories, and non-fiction have been published in Europe, New Zealand, and the United States. In 2011 she published *Transition*, a collection of poems (Les Éditions Madrier). *Blowing Feathers*, a memoir in her mother's voice, came out in 2008 (Lakeview Press). She has served on the editorial committee of the literary journal *Ecrire* and the steering committee of the Geneva Writers' Group (of which she is a founding member). In 2009 she was the editor of *Offshoots*, the biennial anthology of the Geneva Writers' Group.

Ingela Romare, MA, graduated from the C.G. Jung Institute Küsnacht, Zürich in 1997 and since then has maintained a private practice in Malmö, Sweden. She is a training analyst at ISAPZURICH—and also a film director, educated at the Swedish Film Institute from 1965-1968. She has made some fifty documentary films that focus on political, social, and existential topics. One of them, *On the Dignity of the Human Soul*, is about inner imagination helping a person to survive torture and imprisonment. Her film trilogy, *Faith, Hope and Love* was produced in 2004 for Swedish television.

Bernard Sartorius, lic. theol., received his degree in theology from Geneva University in 1965 and afterward worked for several years as a protestant minister. He graduated from the C.G. Jung Institute Zürich in 1974 and maintained his private analytical private first in Geneva, and since 1997 in Lucerne and Zürich. He has been a training analyst at ISAPZURICH since its founding in 2004. Among his many publications are the essays, "Eros and Psyche Revisited" (in *Love: Traversing Its Peaks and Valleys, Jungian Odyssey Series,* Vol. V (New Orleans: Spring Journal and Books, 2013); "La Mecque ou/ou on meurt" (in *Vouivre, Cahiers de psychologie analytique, Pèlerinages,* Numéro 11, 2011); and his book, *L'Eglise Orthodox, Vol. 10 of Grandes religions du monde* (Geneva: Edito-Service, 1982).

Craig E. Stephenson, PhD, is a graduate of the C.G. Jung Institute Zürich, the Institute for Psychodrama (Zumikon, Switzerland), and the Centre for Psychoanalytic Studies, University of Essex. His books include *Possession: Jung's Comparative Anatomy of the Psyche* (Routledge, 2009) and a translation of Luigi Aurigemma's book of essays, *Jungian Perspectives*, from French into English (University of Scranton Press, 2007). He has contributed essays to *The Jung Journal, Cahiers jungiens de psychanalyse, The International Journal for Jungian Studies*, and *Psyche and the City* (Spring

Journal Books, 2010). His new book, *Anteros: A Forgotten Myth*, was published by Routledge in 2011. He is a Jungian analyst in private practice in France.

The 10ᵗʰ Jungian Odyssey

Annual Conference & Retreat

ON THE BRINK

Transitions and Turning Points

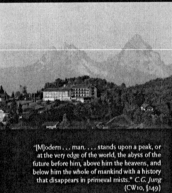

"[M]odern . . . man. . . . stands upon a peak, or at the very edge of the world, the abyss of the future before him, above him the heavens, and below him the whole of mankind with a history that disappears in primeval mists." *C.G. Jung* (CW10, §149)

KEYNOTE SPEAKER
Iain McGilchrist, MD

SPECIAL GUEST
Eva Pattis Zoja, PhD

WITH
Friends & Faculty of ISAPZURICH

May 30 - June 6, 2015
Hotel Seeblick
Emmetten, Switzerland

ISAPZURICH
INTERNATIONAL SCHOOL OF
ANALYTICAL PSYCHOLOGY ZURICH
AGAP POST-GRADUATE JUNGIAN TRAINING

www.jungianodyssey.ch
info@jungianodyssey.ch

Photo: *Bergkulisse* by Christian Perret, with the kind permission of Hotel Seeblick, Emmetten, 2014.

CPSIA information can be obtained at www.ICGtesting.com
Printed in the USA
LVOW10s0825120614

389570LV00005B/309/P